This is the
WEIMARANER

by Ernest H. Hart

Drawings by the author

Distributed in the U.S.A. by T.F.H. Publications, Inc., 211 West Sylvania Avenue, P.O. Box 27, Neptune City, N.J. 07753; in England by T.F.H. (Gt. Britain) Ltd., 13 Nutley Lane, Reigate, Surrey; in Canada to the book store and library trade by Clarke, Irwin & Company, Clarwin House, 791 St. Clair Avenue West, Toronto 10, Ontario; in Canada to the pet trade by Rolf C. Hagen Ltd., 3225 Sartelon Street, Montreal 382, Quebec; in Southeast Asia by Y.W. Ong, 9 Lorong 36 Geylang, Singapore 14; in Australia and the south Pacific by Pet Imports Pty. Ltd., P.O. Box 149, Brookvale 2100, N.S.W., Australia. Published by T.F.H. Publications, Inc. Ltd., The British Crown Colony of Hong Kong.

Frontispiece: Field Ch. Greta von Kallerplatz, S.D.X., owned by Ted and Lori Jarmie.

ISBN 0-87666-406-0

Contents

Cover drawing by Ernest H. Hart.

General instructive photos by Louise Van der Meid.

Ch. Flott von Hausserman

to Lance,
the strong and
silent one.

Foreword

When the Weimaraner first came to our shores, the author became deeply interested in the breed due to its unusual color and the many virtues attributed to it. A good friend, Jack Baird, one of the breed's staunchest supporters, furthered that interest. A short time later, due to my interest in genetic research and through another good friend, Joe Stetson, gun dog editor of *Field and Stream*, I became involved in a small controversy regarding both the color and origin of the Weimaraner. The research I undertook at that time, and rechecked recently, is incorporated in the first chapter of this book.

Through the years my interest in the Gray Ghost has not abated. I have had the good fortune to have hunted behind several fine Weimaraners, and have known the closeness, the rapport, that essence of companionship, that comes to man and dog when sharing an activity that both love. I have seen the Weimaraner in his role as pet and companion in the home and in the obedience ring, where he generally stars, and I have judged him in conformation classes.

Yes, I know the Weimaraner for what he is and what he can give to mankind as a functional symbol of the canine. And because of this knowledge, my most difficult task in writing this book was to be completely objective, to be aloof and coldly analytical in every phase. For, in the face of the breed's early publicity, the almost hysterical accolades heaped upon it and the "super-dog" connotation this brought in its wake, it was imperative that I approach this task with absolute objectivity or destroy the basic reason for this book's being.

This book is for all of you who own, breed, train, hunt, or contemplate the purchase of a Weimaraner. In these pages you will find most of what you will need to know about taking care of your dog in sickness and health, about breeding, feeding, the origin and history, and all else that concerns you and your Weimaraner. You will find here the end results of scientific research in parallel fields, adapted to our own use for our dogs, to aid and better them. For in the pet or hobby field there have been none of the great steps forward in scientific knowledge that there have been in the economic field of animal and plant production for human consumption.

My thanks to all of you who were kind enough to supply me with photographs of your fine Weimaraners. Thanks, also, to Allan H. Hart, D.V.M., for his professional help in the chapter on diseases and first aid.

I hope you enjoy, and benefit from, reading this book, and if through one sentence, one page or chapter, you glean some worth that aids in any small way or helps bring you more understanding of, or pleasure with, your Weimaraner, then the purpose for which this book was conceived has been achieved.

ERNEST H. HART
Orange, Conn.

Chapter I
Origin of the Weimaraner

The story of the relationship between dog and man starts long before the beginnings of recorded history. Anthropologists tell us that dogs played a part in man's life as far back as the end of the Paleolithic period of the Stone Age, perhaps more than 10,000 years ago. This partnership between man and dog is a beneficial one, and the reasons for its beginning are as valid today as they were then. Primitive man found in the dog a beast which could be controlled, whose instincts could be fashioned to conform to his needs: an animal whose natural talents complemented his own. It was fleet where man was slow; it had highly developed scenting ability, and its auditory sense was many times sharper than man's. The dog found and ran down game for man to kill and eat. It helped fight off the ever-present marauding beasts of prey. In return, man protected his dog from the larger carnivores, gave him shelter and food, and tended to his injuries.

Field Ch. Fritz von Wehmann, owned by G. H. and R. G. Wehmann.

And so a pact was formed between man and dog, a partnership that was to endure from the misty beginnings of time down to the present day. For in the dog man had found more than a hunter; he had found a friend, a companion, and a guardian.

It is very likely that hunting dogs were the earliest specialized breed known to man. We cannot, however, be more specific; for the truth is that the early evolution of the hunting dog is hidden in the years to an even greater extent than is the painstakingly traced origin of man. This undeniable fact is as applicable to the gray pointers of Weimar as it is to practically every other canine breed of today.

Shrouded in the mists of time, drowned in a sea of supposition, speculation, and controversial opinion, the origin of the Weimaraner is mostly unknown. Distinct in coloration, it would seem that through this characteristic alone the breed could be traced to its beginning. But even in color theory there is variance of opinion among authorities. An expert on the German Shorthair Pointer, Dr. Paul Kleeman, claimed that the Weimaraner descended from the Great Dane, and that the gray of the Weimaraner was the same color as the "Blue" Great Dane. Major Robert A. D. Herber, called "the father of the

Ch. Gourmet's Sardar, owned and bred by Erma Muster. Sire: Ch. Dok of Fairway; dam: Ch. Silver Linda v. Feldstrom.

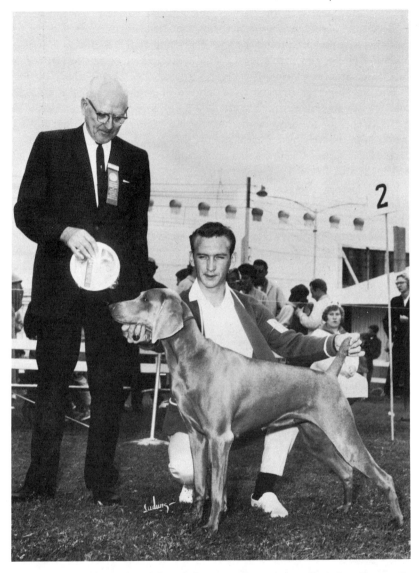

Ch. Kristi von Dottlyle, C.D., P.C., owned and handled by James P. Manley, and bred by James P. Yarborough and Robert P. Richards. Sire: Field Ch. Johann von Kietel, R.D.X., S.D.X.; dam: Madela of Blue Heights. Kristi is shown winning under Dr. Rex Foster. Photo by Joan Ludwig.

breed," and considered the earliest and greatest authority on the breed, in his book, *The Weimaraner,* and the other numerous articles and papers that flowed from his prolific pen proclaimed that the Weimaraner was a mutation within the Brache group and a descendant of the St. Hubertus Brache, or St. Hubert Hound.

The St. Hubertus Brachen were a breed of hounds essentially black in color, which are now extinct but are thought to have played a leading role in the development of many of the hounds and hunting dogs of today. As a matter of fact, a well known scientist and director of the Berlin Zoo, Professor Lutz Heck, named the Brachen as the master strain of hunting dogs from which all other forms descended.

Major Herber theorized that the gray of his beloved breed was a mutation from the black coloration of the St. Hubertus Brachen. In 1931, Dr. N. A. Iljin published a paper dealing with the genetics of coat color inheritance in the Doberman Pinscher, which further advanced the theory of Major Herber. Though some geneticists considered the loss of full black pigmentation in dogs due to an inhibition factor, Dr. Iljin said that "blue" was due to a clumping of the black pigment granules in the outer layer of the hair which resulted in a reduction of the total area covered by black pigment. Hence,

Ch. Gwinner's Thigpenwheel, owned by Julian E. Davidson, and bred by Mildred L. and Billy L. Thigpen. Sire: Ch. Gwinner's Pinweel; dam: Thigpen's Northern Lights. Ditore Studio photo.

Ch. Wetobe's Sandra Bonnet, owned, bred, and handled by Mrs. H. B. Barnett. Sire: Ch. Adam von Gruhlkey; dam: Wetobe's Blue Bonnet, C.D.X. This Weimaraner is shown winning best of opposite sex at the Texas Kennel Club under judge Maxwell Riddle. Photo by Cooksey.

the black coloration becomes somewhat "washed out" or diluted. We know today that a genetic factor for the dilution of pigmentation can be carried by black animals as a recessive, and when two such black dogs are bred together they may produce a "blue."

Dr. Iljin also referred to an "Isabellismus" factor in reference to a silvering effect. Animals carrying this recessive factor of basic body color have been called "Isabellas" by other geneticists. We will return to the "Isabella" later, for the author feels that in this genetic factor lies the secret of the coat color inheritance of the Weimaraner and the one definite clue to the breed's origin.

The famed black St. Hubert hounds of the eighth century were of Celtic origin and were introduced into Germany from France. Major Herber theorized that gray mutations occurred, but were not recognized or written about by sporting men of literature. Again, according to the Major's theory, some astute dog men did favor the gray mutations, bred them together and, in the district of Thuringia near Weimar, gray dogs began to appear in ever increasing numbers and became known, due to the locale, as Weimaraners or Weimar Pointers.

Ch. Kebbena's Rudolf of Bear Creek, owned and bred by William and Margaret Lion. Sire: Ch. Ann's Marty Boy; dam: Johan's Brunhilde. Rudolf is shown in a best of breed win under Dr. Davis. Photo by Page.

Ch. Halann's Woodland Pixie, owned by Herman and Hedy Bolio, and bred by Harold and Ann Hicks. Sire: Ch. Durmar's Karl; dam: Ch. Countess von Van Ness. Photo by Evelyn Shafer.

In 1820, a book on sporting dogs by Winckell published in German mentions "purebred dogs of completely gray or yellow color." These animals were probably early Weimaraners.

Theories on the origin of the breed kept mounting to ever more confusing heights. Dr. A. Stroese, in 1902, declared that "the silver-gray Weimaraner is said to have descended from a yellow and white, smooth-haired English bitch, imported into Germany in the 1820's by the Duke of Weimar and crossbred with German dogs." Another writer who signed his literary efforts "R.F." (assumed to be Robert Fries, Chief Forester) in *Deutsche Waidwerk* No. 19, August 1939, claimed that the Weimaraner originated from purebred, brown German Short-Haired Pointers which had gone through a process of color degenerating or fading. He claimed that through the lack of Vitamin D, silver-gray dogs can be evolved eventually from pure brown animals.

There have been Beagle, Pointer and even Bulldog theories of origin, and an old German writer who signed his name as "Fama," speaks of the old-time hunting dog called a Leithund (Leading Dog) from which was developed the German "Rote Schweissehund," a red-brown dog. And so, with this mass of material and theory at our disposal, we will attempt through the use of analytical genetics to accurately trace the origin of the Weimaraner.

It is undoubtedly true that the St. Hubert hound was the ancestor of the Weimaraner, but only as it was also the ancestor of most of the other hound and sporting breeds. The clue to the real genetic identity of the Weimaraner lies in the words "Red Schweissehund." These dogs were almost certainly derived from the Bloodhound, a breed believed to have come directly from the St. Hubert hound. Indeed, the Red Schweissehund was almost a slightly smaller edition of the Bloodhound.

Now we must go back to Dr. Iljin's "Isabellismus" factor. This genetic recessive, when carried by dogs in the red or tan color series, can produce "Isabella," a dilution of the red factor to a silvery taupe with variation in tone to an almost lavender shade and accompanied by affected pigmentation of eyes, nose, and pads.

The author has seen Redbone Hounds (a breed also possessing Bloodhound ancestry) which were Isabellas and looked very much like undocked Weimaraners.

Here is evidently the coloration source of the "Gray Ghosts" of Weimar; a recessive color inheritance from the Red Schweissehund, which was favored because of its unusual appearance and selected for over the myriad generations of the breed's formation.

Eye color is generally a genetic unit by itself and need not be associated with the hair color of a dog. The type of eye possessed by our Weimaraners was common in Pointers a few generations back and was seen in black and white Pointers as well as liver and whites. The latter often carry yellow or light amber eyes, but the eye color we refer to was called "pearl" and had an entirely different inheritance pattern than the "pearl" or "watch" eyes found in harlequin or merle dogs, and it is definitely a recessive.

In the early days of its existence as a breed, the Weimaraner, sponsored by the sportsmen nobles of the Court of Weimar, was used as a big-game dog, hunting such dangerous quarry as bear, wild boar (always a favorite of men who like the spice of danger added to their hunting forays), wolves, wild cats, and deer. In this capacity the Weimaraners of that day ran like true hounds, picking their scent from the ground, running their game, baying and holding it for the huntsman. These early Gray Ghosts were *not* bird dogs, were *not* pointers, they were hounds like their immediate ancestors. Not long after the breed came into focus, the hunting of big game in Germany, with any regularity, became a rarity, simply because the larger game died out with the encroachment of civilization. But a good combination fur and feather dog, which would own all the qualities the sportsman could want, would be of inestimable value. The breed selected by the nobles of Weimar to fill this role was, of course, the Weimaraner.

Remember though, that the Weimaraner was a hound, not a pointer. How then did they make this drastic change in the breed? By selection for those

Zouave's Knight of Loadstone, S.D.X., owned by Gerald S. Knight. Sire: Von Gaiberg's Zouave; dam: Roger's Diana.

dogs who paused before the quarry and, through generations of selection, molding this characteristic into the breed as it had been done with other pointer breeds? The author thinks not. Not enough generations passed to accomplish this phenomenon. It is much more likely and plausible that Pointer stock was introduced into the Weimaraner breed to shape it into the all-around field dog it is today, and through that pointer stock came the typical eye of the breed along with recessive selection for coat color and other correlated physical aspects of the breed.

It is a recorded fact that Great Danes were used in Weimaraner breeding in an attempt to bring greater size to the breed. German Shorthaired Pointers were also crossed into the breed. In Apolda, a short distance from Weimar, a dog "market," a forerunner of the dog show, was held each year. The group that ran this showing of purebred dogs indicated great interest in the Weimaraner in 1882 and recommended "that cross-breeding of the Weimaraner with the German Pointer be discontinued."

As a matter of fact, the Germans were generally not interested in dog breeding with the same intensity exhibited by the English fanciers who earnestly and knowledgeably bred for purity of type. Because of internal political strife it wasn't until the latter part of the nineteenth century that the

Germans began to seriously breed dogs, and, even then, imported fashionable breeds, especially from England, were given favor over the home-bred products.

Whether the crosses of the gray Weimar dogs to Great Danes and German Pointers are in the direct line of descent of the dogs of today, or whether the animals created by those crosses formed separate lines that eventually died out and had no influence upon the evolution of our modern Weimaraner is open to question. Again, though, there is a genetic clue that adds substance to the theory that Pointers were used in the formation of the breed.

It is well known to sporting dog people that, in the early formation of the pointing breeds short-haired and long-coated animals were bred together. Weimaraner breeders are aware of the long (Setter)-coated puppies that occasionally appear in litters. Wire-haired puppies have also made their appearance in Weimaraner litters in the past. Coats such as these, which depart from the short-haired norm, are caused by the uniting of unrecognized

Aden's Fraulein Ingrid, owned by Robert Aden, and bred by Charles Russel.

Ch. Sandra Silver Knight, owned and bred by Ted Bloomberg. Sire: Ch. Val Knight Ranck: dam; Ch. Sheba von Roda. This bitch is shown scoring best of breed over 71 other entries at the national specialty under judge Earle Adair (left), handler Betty Crawford. Photo by William Brown.

recessives for such coat qualities that are carried in the germ plasm of the breeding partners for generations.*

Where did they come from, these hidden factors that have not manifested themselves for generations behind either dam or sire? They could only come from Pointers that carried the long-coats of setter breeds, or the harsh coats of wire-haired pointing breeds in their heritage. The short-haired coat is dominant and was selected and bred for, but the recessives, lurking in the inheritable material of the breed, are very difficult to wash away.

We can conclude then, that the Weimaraner is directly descended from the Red Schweissehund, and its color is the result of the Isabellismus factor: combined recessives which effect the base coloration. To the basic selected

Throughout his history, the Weimaraner has taken the attention of sportsmen. His past is illustrious, his present position is secure and his future is bright.

hunting breed, at some time in its origin, probably when big game hunting was no longer a part of the German sporting scene, the breeders of the "gray" dogs introduced Pointers to the genetic formula. Selection was then made, by the nobles of Weimar, to mold the breed to the type we know today. The Weimaraner is a breed in which, perhaps more than in any breed extant today, selection was made for recessives to give us the color, type, and characteristics of this noble, different, and intelligent all-purpose sporting dog.

*AUTHOR'S NOTE.—The short-haired coat is dominant. The long coat is purely recessive. Therefore when two long-coated Weimaraners are bred together the result can be nothing but long-coated get. The short-hair, carrying a recessive for long coats, when bred to a short-hair carrying the same hidden characteristic, will produce approximately 25% long coats, 75% short coats. Two-thirds of the short-haired dogs, as well as the long-coated animals, will be carrying genes for long coats.

Chapter II
History of the Weimaraner

As we have seen in our first chapter on the origin of the Weimaraner, the history of this or any breed is not easy to trace. Too much time has elapsed and too many people have been willing to accept and pass on half-truths about the history of their breed that lend it importance and bring to it false romantic values. We can delve into what is known, what is assumed, and by objective research perhaps eventually find the truth or as much of the truth as it is possible to find at this late date.

Ch. Grafmar's Diana, and two of her puppies. She is owned by Jack Baird and was bred by Mrs. Margaret Horn. Sire: Grafmar's Silver Knight; dam: Aura Von Gaiberg. Photo by Annette Samuels.

Grand Duke Karl August, the son of Constantine and Anna Amalia, born in 1757, the year his father died, is said to have been the first of the nobles to own and breed the Gray Ghosts of the sporting gentry. In his day he had great political power and exerted a tremendous influence upon the cultural, political, philosophical, and esthetic life of Thuringia and particularly the city of Weimar, which became known as the "German Athens."

The nobles of his court are said to have developed the Weimaraner dog, but were so jealous of the breed's marvelous attributes that they kept their records secretly so that the gray dog would remain under selective ownership and not become a dog for the masses. This makes a good story, but is scarcely plausible. What probably happened was that the Isabella color phase, a color that could not be held due to its recessive state, but which gave individuality to the breed at a later date, first made its appearance during this period and was adopted by some of the nobles of Weimar.

From a perusal of our first chapter we are aware that Germans of that time were not particularly interested in breeding and establishing pure strains of dogs, as were the English; the Germans gave much greater value to imported breeds than to their native stock. It wasn't until later, in the

Ch. Miss Deborah of Wetobe (left) and Ch. Ring Commander, owned by Mrs. H. B. Barnett, best of opposite sex and best of breed, respectively, at the Weimaraner Club of America, under the late Col. E. E. Ferguson. The dogs are handled by James Rhyan and the owner. Photo by Alexander.

Ch. Leiben's Blitz Angriff, owned by Dr. and Mrs. J. L. Chisler, and bred by Willard J. Spivey. He is shown winning the sporting group at Santa Barbara under judge Virgil Johnson, handler, the late Roland Muller. Photo by Joan Ludwig.

nineteenth century, that the Weimaraner emerged as a definite breed. Then, in 1896, the Delegate Commission (at that time in Germany, an organization similar in scope to our A.K.C.) granted permission to enter Weimaraners in the German Stud Book (established in 1876) and declared them to be an independent and pure breed of dogs.

In 1915 an incident occurred which, more than anything else, helped in bringing the Weimaraner to the forefront of sporting breeds. It was in that year that the sportsman, Major Robert aus der Herber shot over a Weimaraner in the field and immediately became devoted to the breed, a fondness that was to end only with the Major's death in 1946.

Over a period of thirty-one years, this man spread the gospel of the Weimaraner. Writings flowed from his pen in an endless stream and were published in hunting and dog magazines as he waged a one-man crusade for the breed he loved and in which he earnestly believed. He wrote a book, *The Weimaraner*, and became *the* authority on the "Gray Dogs." He came to be known affectionately and in acknowledgement of his years of work as "the father of the breed."

He became president of the German Weimaraner Club in 1921 and through his efforts the Weimaraner gained world-wide recognition and popularity. Major Herber's good friend, E. von Otto, a publisher and dog-show judge, was also one of those who helped the growth of the Weimaraner, though he was, like Dr. Paul Kleeman, who evolved his own theory on the origin of the Weimaraner, essentially interested in the German Shorthaired Pointer. Dr. Kleeman was president of the Berlin Stud Club for many years and the outstanding authority on German Shorthairs in the world during his time.

Weimaraners were introduced to Austria in 1913 when Otto von Stockmayer imported a dog of the breed for Prince Hans von Ratibor. The Prince was seeking a new and better breed of all-around hunting dog for his estate, Grafenegg, and he found what he wanted in the Weimaraner. He became the first president of the Weimaraner Club of Austria and his influence upon selectivity of ownership of the breed was reflected in both Germany and Austria.

A valuable addition to our knowledge of the history of the breed was supplied by J. Carl Linke, who wrote that he had seen Weimaraners in the dog market at Apolda in the early 1870's and thought that they came from

Ch. Eilatan's Valdusk, C. D., owned by Don and Marge Fannell, and bred by William J. Hutchins. Sire: Ch. Val Knight Ranck; dam: Ch. Mischievous Misty, U.D.T.

Ch. Leer's Jan Tomerlin, S.D.X., R.D.X., owned by W. S. Tomerlin and bred by M. E. Leer. Sire Ch. Burt v.d. Harrasburg; dam: Ch. Tamara Frederica. This Weimaraner has scored impressively during her show career under the handling of Jack Dexter. Photo by Joan Ludwig.

that neighborhood. He mentions the fact that in the early years they looked like gray Bloodhounds, but changed as the time passed.

The Weimaraner Club of Germany, founded in 1897 at Erfurt, Thuringia, jealously controls the breeding program of the Weimaraner and restricts, through selection, those who are allowed to join the club and own a specimen of the breed.

In 1935, in agreement with the Austrian breed club, the Weimaraner Club of Germany adopted the following standard:

This breed is the only Short-haired Pointer breed of Germany which succeeded in remaining unmixed. (Uncrossed.)

GENERAL APPEARANCE—Altogether noble appearance; beautiful shape; sinewy; intelligent expression. Medium sized, height between 56-74

Ch. Gwinner's Pinwheel, owned and bred by Tony P. and Beatrice S. Gwinner, and handled by Mr. Gwinner. Sire: Ch. Johnson's Arco v.d. Auger; dam: Ch. Cati v.d. Gretchenhof. Pinwheel is one of the top winners in the breed. He is shown winning best of breed over 110 dogs at the Weimaraner Club of America under James W. Trullinger. Photo by Alexander.

centimeters [22-29 inches]. Bitch a little smaller [lower] than dog.

HEAD—In accordance with the size of the body, more often narrow than broad; dog a little broader than bitch. In the center of the head a small groove, occipital bone protruding slightly. Corner teeth long without being pointed. Back of the nose [muzzle] straight; often slightly arched, never sagging upwards. Extremely small gap [stop] in front of the forehead; lips hanging over moderately; small mouth wrinkle. Cheek muscles distinctly marked, because attached at the back. Dry head.

LEATHER—[Lopears]. Broad, rounded off in a point, slightly turned when at attention; when put forward, at approximately same level as corner of mouth; high and narrow attached.

NOSE—Dark flesh colored turning to purple and gradually into gray.

EYES—Color of amber, with intelligent expression.

BACK—A somewhat longish back, as long as it shows no downward inclination, is characteristic of the breed; not to be regarded as faulty.

TAIL—When not cropped, long, hanging down almost vertically, point bent slightly backwards. Thickness of tail in accordance with shape of body.

LEGS—Sinewy: upper arm well angled; pastern almost straight; paws well closed.

COAT—Soft to the touch; denser than with other short-haired breeds; underside (brisket) slightly less thick. Coarser hair is not faulty.

COLOR—Silver-, deer-, or mouse-gray; head and leather mostly a little lighter; white markings in small measure, mostly on the chest, are neither ugly nor faulty since also characteristic of the breed. Neither is the reddish-yellow shade on the head or legs, which nowadays occurs seldom, to be regarded as a fault; however, a Weimaraner with reddish-yellow coloring should not receive more than "good" when tested for his shape. If outstanding for hunting purposes he should not be excluded from breeding. Along the middle of the back there is often a dark eel-stripe.

Notice: Very occasionally there are some long-haired Weimaraners. They have a right to be listed, provided their origin can be traced back undeniably until the fourth generation. One should strive to raise such long-haired Weimaraners. Approximately four vertebrae only should be cropped from the tail.

Meanwhile, in Austria, under the sponsorship of Prince Hans von Ratibor, the Weimaraner became the leading sporting dog. The Prince's enthusiasm for the breed knew no bounds. He instigated training courses and trials on his own preserves and these became social as well as sporting events.

The German and Austrian clubs were very close, working together and aiding each other in all the phases necessary to advance and help the breeding and working of the Gray Ghosts.

It must be realized that control of a breed in Germany is much more rigid

Ch. Countess von Van Ness, owned by Harold and Ann Hicks and bred by Harry T. and Georgia E. Luthy. She is shown scoring best of opposite sex at the Weimaraner Club of America, under judge Harry A. McCauley, handler, Don Bradley. Photo by Evelyn Shafer.

than it can be in this country. There breed wardens suggest breedings to be made, check the stock and the puppies during their growth period, and allow only a limited number of seven puppies to a litter—the rest must be culled and killed. Breeders who defy the club and its wardens and make breedings that are not recommended are not allowed to register the breeding results, thus both stock and owners of Weimaraners are rigidly selected and kept at a minimum.

The Weimaraner Club stresses the worth of the breed as a sporting dog essentially. During Hitler's rule and World War II, membership became even more exclusive. The Club was practically disorganized for a long time after the end of the war until Allied restrictions were lifted from Germany.

Weimaraners, like many other German breeds, were bred in quantity during Allied occupation and sold for whatever the traffic would bear to be exported by the occupation forces. But when the club began to function again, this practice was stopped and a rule made that only half of any litter could be sold to foreign buyers. The club also initiated a system, *Zuchtwertnachweis*, for evaluating a dog's eligibility for breeding. These are comprehensive questionnaires kept on file with the Club. A member who does not follow instructions completely in filling out the questionnaire is severely penalized.

When German sportsmen were granted permission, in 1952, to hunt again, the Club instituted a series of field trials specifically to test every dog's worth in the field. These dogs are also given basic *Schutzhund* (obedience and protection) training.

Hellas Blaze Adventure, owned by Duane E. Dankert, and bred by Kenneth and Frances Johnson. Sire: Blader von Frick; dam: Gretchen's Heidi Golden Girl. Blaze has distinguished himself by placing in and winning field trials all throughout the Middle West. Photo by Harry Hill.

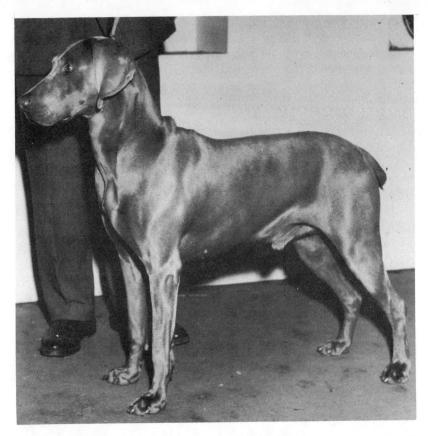

Sh. Ch. Monroes Dynamic, owned by Mrs. J. I. Matuszcwska (England).
Photo by C. M. Cooke and Son.

INTRODUCTION TO ENGLAND

Following World War II, Major Eric Richardson and Major Bob Petty, officers in the Army of Occupation in Germany, heard about a breed of super-dogs unknown in England. These dogs were Weimaraners and the British officers were intrigued by a breed that they were told would work on fur or feather, as hound or pointer, or as a retriever on land or in water, and was the equal or more of any breed as guard dog or house pet and companion.

Fascinated, the two officers attempted to purchase stock to import to England and establish the breed there. It was two years before they were able to buy any stock, but by the time they returned home each owned a pair of Weimaraners. The bitches were bred and whelped their litters on English soil.

A club was formed similar in scope and activity to the German and Austrian clubs. Bitches are not allowed to be bred but once a year and must be past their second season. In Germany and Austria it is a rule that bitches must not be serviced before their third season. Strangely enough, in its standard for the breed, the Weimaraner Club of Great Britain advances a theory proposing that the Gray Ghost may well be of Russian origin.

THE GRAY GHOST IN AMERICA

The name "Gray Ghost" for the Weimaraner evidently evolved in this country. Some sportsman of vivid imagination and a pretty taste for descriptive phraseology may have watched his Weimaraner float ghostlike through wisps of early morning mist, quartering a field, and the nickname leaped unbidden to his mind as most descriptive of the glorious sight.

The breed was introduced to America by an ardent sportsman, Howard Knight, of Providence, R.I. Knight met Fritz Grossman, who was visiting the United States from Germany in 1928. While indulging in their mutual hobby of hunting, Grossman mentioned the Weimaraner. Extremely interested in the new (to him) breed, Knight applied for membership in the

Ch. Elge of Belle Creek, owned by George L. and Eleanor E. Burmeister, and bred by M. Pinto. Sire: Ch. Dan's Ricky of Rockledge; dam: Constant Germain. This Weimaraner is a national specialty winner.

Ch. Crook 'N' Nanny's Silver Thor, S.D., owned by Marie Seidelman and bred by Jean Budler. Thor is an accomplished field performer as well as a winner on the show bench. He is shown in a win under judge Hollis Wilson, handled by Rich Milke. Photo by Ritter.

German club. Subsequently, after pressure by Grossman, the American was accepted and, in 1929, received a pair of three-year-old, trained hunting and retrieving Weimaraners from Germany selected for him by Grossman.

Before he received the dogs, Knight had to swear never to cross any other breed into the pure lines of the Weimaraner and to protect the breed in every way possible from deterioration. This almost hysterical pledge was most ironic in the light of what followed, for it was found that the pair of dogs Knight had received from Germany, unknown to Grossman, had been deliberately made sterile by their original owners.

But the American sportsman was so impressed by the pair of animals, sterile though they were, that he arranged to import others that were able to reproduce. One of these was an imported puppy whose name, Mars aus der Wulfsriede, appears in many American pedigrees today. This dog was bred by Major Herber, who also sent Knight a lovely bitch, Dorle v. Schwarzen Kamp, as a gift.

During the early days of the breed in America so many superlatives were attached to the Weimaraner's abilities by owners and breeders that it was considered, by many, to be a super-dog possessed of unlimited powers. No breed of dogs, no matter how great, could live up to such ridiculous publicity.

Ch. Wolfsburg's Lobo, owned by Redhill Kennels and bred by C.M. Gisel and S. D. Enochs. Sire: Ch. Alfo v. Wolfsburg; dam: Jet Smoke Logan. Handler: R. Kelton.

The result was that the breed fell into a short period of decline before interest in it leveled off and the Weimaraner became recognized by sportsmen for its own very real inherent abilities in the home and the field.

At the beginning, Weimaraners were scarce in this country and were sold at fabulously high prices and only to those who had been admitted to the very exclusive Weimaraner Club, which followed closely the precepts of the German parent club.

Knight did not sell any dogs. He preferred to give them to a few interested friends. Later, when he gave up hunting, he presented his stock to Mr. and Mrs. A. F. Horn of Grafmar Kennels, breeders of fine German Shepherd dogs. The Weimaraner Club, formed at this time, looked to this nucleus of animals to give the breed its initial start in this country.

Ch. Dawnee's Donner von Sturm, owned by William Diemunsch, and bred by Lillian and Edward Larsen. Sire: Ch. Elsmere's Baron von Sturm; dam: Dawnee's Silver Sheen Dutchess. This dog is handled in the ring by his co-breeder Edward Larsen, with whom he is pictured. Photo by Stewart.

Ch. Val Knight Ranck, owned by John Boehne, and bred by Wesley A.
Ranck. He is shown winning first in the sporting group at the Westminster
Kennel Club under judge William Lubben, handler, Tom Crowe. This
typical male has been one of the top winners and producers of the breed.
Photo by Evelyn Shafer.

These dogs, acquired from Howard Knight and then bred by Mr. and Mrs.
Horn, were Adda v. Schwarzen Kamp, Dorle v. Schwarzen Kamp (sister to
Adda), Aura v. Gaiberg, and Mars aus der Wulfsriede. These animals formed
the basis of the breed in America. Later, in 1948, new imports arrived on our
shores to enrich the lines so carefully used and guarded here.

The earlier fanciers of the breed formed and acted as officers and governors
of the Weimaraner Club of America, which held its first annual meeting in
Boston, Mass., on February 21, 1943, approximately two months after the
Weimaraner was recognized and accepted as a breed by the A.K.C.

These fanciers, fine dog people all, were Howard Knight, Darwin S. Morse,

Mrs. Gertrude Warwich, Mrs. A. F. Horn, Mrs. Frank E. Barton, Arthur C. Elsholtz, and Jack Baird, then vice-president of the Weimaraner Club. An official breed standard was published and later revised. Among these early and enthusiastic fanciers must also be listed William Olson, Harold Goldsmith, Charlotte Sibley, Paul A. Kolb, Mrs. Richard L. Bonnell, Helen Peck, R. E. Schoenberg, Darwin S. Morse and Reverend and Mrs. Eric N. Lindblade.

After the breed had become established in the United States, Canadian fanciers looked, liked what they saw, and established their own Weimaraner Club, importing dogs from the States as a nucleus. The first dogs of the breed registered in Canada, in 1948, were owned by Frank Bush and Mathew L. Sterzer, who brought from Germany a mature stud, Ajax v. Reiningen, to introduce new genetic material to the stock brought to Canada from the U.S. Canada undoubtedly now possesses some of the finest strains of Weimaraner breeding available.

As in the United States, Canada went through its period of hysterical

Ch. Valhalla's Gray Majesty, owned and handled by Don Button, and bred by Albert M. Greenfield, Jr. Sire: Ch. Gray Majesty; dam: Ch. Valhalla's Silver Accolade. Val is shown going best of winners at the Weimaraner Club of America to finish his championship, under judge Charles Siever.

claiming of attributes for the breed that could never exist in any canine. But, after a wild breeding period launched by unscrupulous dog jockeys interested only in profit, breeding leveled off, the hysteria over the new breed abated, and a healthy era of good breeding and no-nonsense interest in the breed followed.

In the United States, in 1952, a Weimaraner, Champion Burt v.d. Harrasburg (Imp.), won a Best in Show, the first for the breed: Champion Deal's Sporting True Aim II, by an imported brother of Burt's and out of Champion Grafmar's Dove, won Best of Breed at the Westminster Kennel Club Show in Madison Square Garden, repeating at Morris and Essex, 1952 and 1953, and second in the Sporting Group at the Garden. Then he took Best in Show at Framingham, Mass. The Gray Ghost, bred to a point of major quality, has done its share of show winning throughout the country. As a competitor in obedience trials, the Weimaraner is excellent also.

As time passes, the Weimaraner is gaining more and more recognition as a field trial performer due to an increasing interest in this area of activity by American owners and breeders. Essentially the breed was used by sportsmen as private hunting dogs and it was several years before "Gray Ghosts" began to make their appearance at field trials.

The Weimaraner fills a very real need in the hearts of dog lovers, breeders, and hunters. He can and will do most anything any other breed can do and do it well. His temperament and trainability make him an excellent watchdog, home companion and children's pal. He is a superlative obedience dog and a fine hunting dog for fur or feather, on land or in water.

The Weimaraner is not a kennel dog. He does best when allowed to share in family life as a responsible member of the family. The Gray Ghost's popularity, his exalted status in the family of canine breeds throughout the world, is assured and it is certain that this dog, bred by nobles for a noble purpose, will always fill the hearts and minds of all men with its grace, its intelligence and its unusual beauty.

Chapter III
The Riddle of Inheritance

Before we begin to delve into the riddle of inheritance, we must first clear away the debris of old untruths and superstition so that we may see clearly the true structure that lies beyond. The inheritance of acquired characteristics is one of the fallacious theories that was widely believed and has its disciples even today. Birthmarking is another false theory which must be discarded in the light of present-day genetic knowledge. The genes which give our dogs all their inheritable material are isolated in the body from almost all environmental influence, except high levels of radioactivity. What the host does or has done to him influences them not at all. The so-called "proofs" advanced by the adherents of both these bogus theories were simply isolated coincidences.

Telegony is another of the untrue beliefs about influencing inherited characteristics. This is the theory that the sire of one litter could or would influence the progeny of a future litter out of the same bitch, but sired by an entirely different stud. Telegony is, in its essence, comparable to the theory of saturation, which is the belief that if a bitch is bred many times in succession to the same stud, she will become so "saturated" with his "blood" that she will produce only puppies of his type, even when mated to an entirely different stud. By far the strongest and most widely believed was the theory that the blood was the vehicle through which all inheritable material was passed from parents to offspring, from one generation to the next. The taint of this error still persists in the phraseology we employ in our breeding terms, such as "bloodlines," "percentage of blood," "pure-blooded," "blue-blooded," etc.

The truth was found in spite of such persistent theories, and in the history of science there is no more dramatic story, than that of the discovery of the true method of inheritance. No, the truth was not arrived at in some fine endowed scientific laboratory gleaming with the mysterious implements of research. The scene was instead a small dirt garden in Moravia, which is now a part of Czechoslovakia. Here Gregor Johann Mendel, an Augustinian monk, planted and crossed several varieties of common garden peas and quietly recorded the differences that occurred through several generations. Over a

Ch. Helmanhof's Storm Cloud, U.D., owned by Mrs. Helms Crutchfiled, and bred by Mrs. Hazel Lampkin. Sire: Grafmar's Ador, C.D.; dam: Silver Blue Sue. Stormy was the first group winner in the breed, and made friends for the breed far and wide when relatively few people were acquainted with Weimaraners. Drawing by Peg Johnson. Photo by Annette Samuels.

period of eight years this remarkable man continued his studies. Then, in 1865, he read a paper he had prepared regarding his experiments to the local Brunn Society, a group of historians and naturalists. The Society subsequently published this paper in its journal, which was obscure and definitely limited in distribution.

Now we come to the amazing part of this story, for Mendel's theory of inheritance, which contained the fundamental laws upon which all modern advances in genetics have been based, gathered dust for thirty-four years, and it seemed that one of the most important scientific discoveries of the nineteenth century was to be lost to mankind. Then in 1900, sixteen years after Mendel's death, the paper was rediscovered and his great work given to the world.

Ch. Shadowmar Barthaus Dorilio, owned, bred, and handled by Dorothy Remensnyder. Sire: Ch. Von Gaiberg's Nordsee Ponto; dam: Ch. Shadowmar Little Kate. This dog is a specialty, group and best in show winner. Photo by Evelyn Shafer.

In his experiments with the breeding of garden peas, Mendel correctly determined the units of heredity. He found that when two individual plants which differed in a unit trait were mated, one trait appeared in the offspring and one did not. The trait which was visible he named the "dominant" trait, and the one which was not visible he called the "recessive" trait. He proposed that traits, such as color, are transmitted by means of units in the sex cells and that one of these units must be pure, let us say either black or white, but never be a mixture of both. From a black parent which is pure for that trait, only black units are transmitted, and from a white parent, only white

MENDELIAN EXPECTATION CHART
The six possible ways in which a pair of determiners can unite. Ratios apply to expectancy over large numbers, except in lines no. 1, 2 and 6 where exact expectancy is realized in every litter.

units can be passed down. But when one parent is black and one is white, a hybrid occurs which transmits both the black and white units in equal amounts. The hybrid itself will take the color of the dominant parent, yet carry the other color as a recessive. Various combinations of unit crosses were tried by Mendel, and he found that there were six possible breeding combinations with regard to a simple trait. The chart shows how this law of Mendel's operates and the expected results. This simple Mendelian law holds true in the sexual breeding of all living things: plants, mice, humans, or Weimaraners.

The beginning of new life in animals arises from the union of a male sperm and a female egg cell. Each sperm cell has a nucleus containing one set of chromosomes, which are small packages, or units, of inheritable material. Each egg also possesses a nucleus of one set of chromosomes. The new life formed by the union of sperm cell and egg cell then possesses two sets of chromosomes: one from the sperm, one from the egg, or one set from the sire and one set from the dam. For when the sperm cell enters the egg, it does two things: it starts the egg developing and it adds a set of chromosomes to the set already in the egg. Here is the secret of heredity. For in the chromosomes lie the genes that shape the destiny of the unborn young. Thus we see that the pattern of heredity, physical and mental, is transmitted to our dog from its sire and dam through tiny units called genes, which are the connecting links between the puppy and his ancestors. The basic governing entity determining heredity is a large molecule known as deoxyribonucleic acid or DNA. DNA bulks large in present day genetic research, for it is believed to be the guiding force behind specific cell growth. DNA, like a chemical Svengali, uses cells for its Trilby, giving commands which the cells

Ch. Aura von Hausserman, owned and bred by Mr. and Mrs. Adolph Hausserman. Sire: Ch. Flott von Haimberg (imported); dam: Arcin's Hella von Hausserman. She is shown with her handler Fritz Mueller and some of her winnings.

Ch. Tom's Gray Flash, owned by Thomas and Esther Versele, and bred by William Rouschman. Sire: King von Romulus; dam: Queen von Romulus. Flash is shown scoring under judge J. J. Duncan, with Horace Hollands, handling. Photo by Norton of Kent.

are powerless to resist. Geneticists now believe that DNA exists in all living things, which are but vehicles for DNA's constant reproduction of more DNA.

The packets of genes, the chromosomes, resemble long, paired strings of beads. Each pair is alike, the partners formed the same, yet differing from the like partners of the next pair. In the male mammal we find the exception to this rule, for here there is one pair of chromosomes composed of two that are not alike. These are the sex chromosomes, and in the male they are different from those in the female in that the female possesses a like pair while the male does not. If we designate the female chromosomes as X, then the female pair is XX. The male too has an X chromosome, but its partner is a Y chromosome. If the male X chromosome unites with the female X chromosome, then the resulting embryo will be a female. But if the male Y chromosome is carried by the particular sperm that fertilizes the female egg, the resulting progeny will be a male. It is, therefore, a matter of chance as to what sex the offspring will be, since fertilization is random.

The actual embryonic growth of the puppy is a process of division of cells to form more and more new cells, and at each cell division of the fertilized egg each of the two sets of chromosomes provided by sire and dam also divide, until all the myriad divisions of cells and chromosomes have reached an amount necessary to form a complete and living entity. Then birth becomes an accomplished fact, and we see before us a living, squealing Weimaraner puppy.

What is he like, this puppy? He is what his controlling genes have made him. His sire and dam have contributed one gene of each kind to their puppy, and this gene which they have given him is but one of the two which each parent possesses for a particular characteristic. Since he has drawn these determiners at random, they can be either dominant or recessive genes. His dominant heritage we can see when he develops, but what he possesses in recessive traits is hidden.

There are rules governing dominant and recessive traits useful in summarizing what is known of the subject at the present time. We can be reasonably sure that a dominant trait: (1) Does not skip a generation. (2) Will affect a relatively large number of the progeny. (3) Will be carried only by the affected individuals. (4) Will minimize the danger of continuing undesirable characteristics in a strain. (5) Will make the breeding formula of each individual quite certain.

With recessive traits we note that: (1) The trait may skip one or more generations. (2) On the average a relatively small percentage of the individuals in the strain will show the trait. (3) Only those individuals which carry a pair of determiners for the trait, exhibit it. (4) Individuals carrying only one determiner can be ascertained only by mating. (5) The trait, to be manifested, must come through both sire and dam.

You will hear some breeders say that the bitch contributes sixty percent or more to the excellence of the puppies. Others swear that the influence of the sire is greater than that of the dam. Actually, the puppy receives fifty percent of his germ plasm from each, though one parent may be so dominant that it seems that the puppy received most of his inheritable material from that parent. From the fact that the puppy's parents also both received but one set of determiners from each of their parents and in turn have passed on but one of their sets to the puppy, it would seem that one of those sets that the

Chromosomes in nucleus of cell.

Chromosomes arranged in pairs, showing partnership.

grandparents contributed has been lost and that therefore the puppy has inherited the germ plasm from only two of its grandparents, not four. But chromosomes cross over and exchange segments, and it is possible for the puppy's four grandparents to contribute an equal 25 per cent of all the genes inherited, or various and individual percentages, one grandparent contributing more and another less. It is even possible for the puppy to inherit no genes at all from one grandparent and fifty percent from another.

The genes that have fashioned this puppy of ours are of chemical composition and are living cells securely isolated from nearly all outside influences, a point which we have made before and which bears repeating. Only certain kinds of man-directed radiation, some poisons or other unnatural means can cause change in the genes. Environment can affect an individual, but not his germ plasm. For instance, if the puppy's nutritional needs are not fully provided for during his period of growth, his end potential will not be attained, but regardless of his outward appearance, his germ plasm remains inviolate and capable of passing on to the next generation the potential that was denied him by proper feeding.

Breeding fine dogs would be a simple procedure if all characteristics were governed by simple Mendelian factors, but alas, this is not so. Single genes are not solely responsible for single characteristics, mental or physical. The complexity of any part of the body and its dependence upon other parts in order to function properly makes it obvious that we must deal with interlocking blocks of controlling genes in a life pattern of chain reaction. Eye color, for instance, is determined by a simple genetic factor, but the ability to see, the complicated mechanism of the eye, the nerves, the blood supply, the retina and iris, even how your Weimaraner reacts to what he sees, are all part of the genetic pattern of which eye color is but a segment.

Since the genes are chemical structures, they can and do change, or mutate. In fact, it is thought now that many more gene mutations take place than

Ch. Warhorse Billy of Redhill, C.D., owned by Redhill Kennels, and bred by Darryl and Brent Keener. Sire: Ch. Wolfsburg's Lobo; dam: Perry's Silver Czarina. This fine male is shown winning the sporting group at the Silver Bay Kennel Club under judge Virgil Johnson, the late Roland Muller, handler. Photo by Joan Ludwig.

Wetobe's Blue Bonnet, owned and handled by Mrs. H. B. Barnett, shown in a best of breed win under judge Herman G. Cox. This is a rare blue Weimaraner.

were formerly suspected, but that the great majority are either within the animal, where they cannot be seen, or are so small in general scope that they are overlooked. The dramatic mutations which affect the surface are the ones we notice and select for or against according to whether they direct us toward our goal or away from it. Again, with the vagary inherent in all living things, a mutated gene can change back to the original form.

It is interesting to note that genetic studies of the fruit fly indicate that about one quarter of all mutations are lethal or debilitating. Sterility is produced in one or both of the sexes in approximately fifteen to twenty percent of all fruit fly mutations, and there is a varied reduction of vitality and vigor in almost all new mutations. These are spontaneous mutations, from natural causes.

Examples of mutations in dogs are the albino German Shepherd, pure white and with pink eyes and nose, and the pure black German Shepherd. A male and female albino when bred together cannot produce any but albino young. Similarly, when two pure blacks are bred, they produce only black young.

We see then that a puppy is the product of his germ plasm, which has been handed down from generation to generation. We know that there are certain rules that generally govern the pattern that the genes form, and that a gene which prevents another gene from showing its effects in an individual is said to be a dominant and the repressed gene a recessive. Remember, the animal itself is not dominant or recessive in color or any other characteristic. It is the gene that is dominant or recessive, as judged by results. We find that an animal can contain in each of his body cells a dominant and a recessive gene. When this occurs, the dog is said to be heterozygous. As illustrated in the chart in this chapter, we know that in contrast to the heterozygous individual, there are animals which contain two genes of the same kind in their cells—either two dominants or two recessives—and these animals are said to be homozygous. There are four factors that cause change by breaking genetic equilibrium in a population of animals: mutation, selection, migration, genetic drift. In our controlled breeding of dogs, we are concerned only with the first two factors.

Ch. Norman's Nifty Nina, owned by Robert and Cynthia Gronbach, and bred by Norman LeBoeuf. Sire: Ch. Ann's Ricky Boy, Jr.; dam: Ch. Ann's Merrylande Bounce. Nina is the dam of the notable Winner, Ch. Gronbach's Aladdin, C.D., and is handled by her owner. Photo by William Brown.

Ch. Holly Austa Fawn, owned by George L. and Eleanor E. Burmeister, and bred by Ray and Marie Masse. Sire: Ch. Ann's Rickey Boy; dam: Ch. Masse's Cynda Aus Der Grau. This bitch was twice best of opposite sex at the Westminster Kennel Club show.

Every bitch that stands before us, every stud we intend to use, is not just one dog, but two. Every living thing is a Jekyll and Hyde, shadow and substance. The substance is the Weimaraner that lives and breathes and moves before us, the animal that we see, the physical manifestation of the interaction of genetic characters and environment: the "phenotype." The shadow is the Weimaraner we don't see, yet this shadow is as much a part of the dog before us as the animal we see. This shadow-Weimaraner is the gene-complex, or total collection of genes: the "genotype." The visual substance is easily evaluated, but the invisible shadow must also be clearly seen and evaluated, for both shadow and substance equally contribute to the generations to come. Without understanding the complete genetic picture of any particular dog, we cannot hope to successfully use that dog to accomplish specific results. In order to understand, we must delve into the genetic background of the animal's ancestry until the shadow becomes as clearly discernible as the substance and we can evaluate the dog's genetic worth as a whole; for this dog that stands before us is but the containing vessel, the custodian of a specific pattern of heredity.

We have tried to present to you a working knowledge of the process of inheritance, picking the most pertinent aspects from the great amount of literature pertaining to this subject. If you wish to delve deeper into this most fascinating of all sciences, you will find in the bibliography books of much greater scope than we could cram into this one chapter. But before we leave the subject, one more important phase must be examined. This is the relationship of animal to man in regard to genetics. Though man is an animal and follows the pattern of genetic inheritance precisely as the lower animals do, we must not fashion a parallel between the two. Animals have only biological heredity, while man is greatly influenced by a very complicated

Klug's Velvet Shadow, owned by Don Klug and bred by Charles Russell. This dog is typical of Weimaraners used all over the United States as top-drawer shooting dogs.

and demanding cultural or social inheritance. In our breeding operations we can select, but man does not, and the mesh of civilization which he has woven around himself does not allow for natural selection except in extreme cases. Though social inheritance is not transmitted through the chromosomes, being an acquired characteristic, it is nevertheless linked with inheritance in that it is absorbed by the reasoning human brain. Here is the great difference between man and animal. Man can reason and invent, the animal cannot. Man conquers environment through imagination, reasoning, and invention; the animal either dies or adapts itself through changes in function and bodily structure.

The study of genetics still goes on, as men of science delve deeper and deeper into cause and effect. What we know today of inheritance is of immeasurable importance in animal breeding, removing a great deal of the guesswork from our operations. Yet we do not know enough to make the breeding of top stock a cut-and-dried matter, or to reduce it to the realm of pure science, with a definite answer to every problem. Perhaps this is where the fascination lies. Life is spontaneous and many times unstable, so that even with the greater knowledge that the future will no doubt bring, it is possible that the breeding of top animals will still remain a combination of science and art, with a touch of necessary genius and esthetic innovation, to ever lend fascination to this riddle of inheritance.

Chapter IV
The Roots of Breeding

In today's mechanistic world, with its rushing pace and easy pleasures, much of the creative urge in man has been throttled. We who breed dogs are extremely fortunate, for in our work we have a real creative outlet—we are in the position of being able to mold beauty and utility in living flesh and blood. Our tools are the genes of inheritance, and our art, their infinite combination. We have the power to create a work of art that will show the evidence of our touch for generations to come.

Now that we have absorbed some of the basic facts of heredity, we can, with greater understanding, examine the various kinds of breeding that can be used in perpetuating wanted characteristics. We have learned that within the design of the germ plasm great variation occurs. But within the breed itself as a whole, we have an average, or norm, which the great majority of Weimaraners mirror. Draw a straight horizontal line on a piece of paper and label this line, "norm." Above this line draw another and label it, "above norm." This latter line represents the top dogs, the great ones, and the length of this line will be very much shorter than the length of the "norm" line. Below the "norm" line draw still another line, designating this to be, "below norm." These are the animals possessing faults which we do not wish to perpetuate.

Since the time of the first registered Weimaraners, the number of breeders who have molded the characteristics of the breed both here and abroad have been legion. Many of these Weimaraners were bred without a basic knowledge of any of the fundamentals. The real objective of breeding, however, is to raise the norm of a given breed and thereby approach always closer to the breed standard.

If we are to achieve the greatest good from any program of breeding, there are four important traits which we must examine. It is essential that these traits should never depart from the norm.

The first is fertility. The lack of this essential in any degree must be guarded against diligently.

The second is vigor. Loss of vigor, or hardiness, and its allied ills, such as lowered resistance to disease, finicky eating, etc., will lead to disaster.

The roots of breeding are reflected in the fruits of breeding, or puppies, such as these. The breeder is a craftsman of dogflesh and must utilize the scientific and practical knowledge of dog breeding to bring forth "canine masterpieces." Photo by Annette Samuels.

Longevity is the third important trait. An individual of great worth, who represents a fortunate combination of excellent characteristics which he dominantly passes on to his offspring, must be useful for a long time after his or her worth is recognized by the progeny produced.

The fourth is temperament. Here is the sum total of the dog's usefulness to man in the various categories in which he serves. Lack of true Weimaraner character nullifies any other advances which you may make in your breeding program.

The norm can be likened to the force of gravity, possessing a powerful pull toward itself, so that regression toward the average is strong, even though you have used in your breeding parents which are both above average. The same holds true for progeny bred from animals below norm, but from these you will get a lesser number which reach the mean average and a greater number which remain below norm. In the case of the better-than-average parents, some of the progeny will stay above the norm line and the majority will regress. Occasionally a dog of superior structure is produced by a poor family, but inevitably this animal is useless as a stud because he will produce all his objectionable family traits and none of the fortuitous

Ch. Wilhelm Von Fulda, U.D., S.D.X., R.D.X., owned by Richard W. Smith, Cdr. CEC, USN (ret). Sire Dual Ch. Baron Von Randolph, U.D., S.D.X., R.D.X., T.D.; dam: Debutante Miss Deborah, C.D. Wilhelm has distinguished himself on the bench, in obedience, and afield; truly an all-round dog, as was his sire before him.

Despite modern breeding methods and new knowledge, the science of genetics is still unpredictable. An inferior member of a litter can produce better puppies than a top winning brother or sister. Photo by Louise Van der Meid.

characteristics he displays in himself. From a breeding standpoint it is far better to use an average individual from top stock than a top individual from average or below-average stock. It is also true that many times a great show dog produces average progeny while his little-known brother, obscured by the shadow of the great dog's eminence, produces many above-average young. This is not as strange as it sounds when we consider the fact that the individual animal is the custodian of his germ plasm and it is this germ plasm that produces, not the individual. In this instance, due to variation in the germ plasm, the top dog does not possess the happy genetic combinations that his average brother does and so cannot produce stock of comparative value.

Ch. Crook 'N' Nanny's Silver Adonis, S.D., owned by Rich Milke (handling) and Marie Seidelman, and bred by Jean Budler. Sire: Ch. Alex of Happy Days; dam: Duchess Florian Grey. Adonis is shown in a win under Forrest Hall. Photo by Frasie.

Any of the various categories of breeding practice which we will outline can be followed for the betterment of the breed if used intelligently. Regardless of which practice one follows, there generally comes a time when it is necessary to incorporate one or more of the other forms into the breeding program in order to concentrate certain genetic characters, or to introduce new ones which are imperative for over-all balance. Outcross breeding is not recommended as a consistent practice. Rather, it is a valuable adjunct to the other methods when used as a corrective measure. Yet outcross breeding in the Weimaraner does not, as would be supposed from definition, produce completely heterozygous young. The root stock of the breed is the same regardless of which breeding partners are used, and much of the stock which represents what we term outcross breeding shows common ancestry within a few generations.

INBREEDING

By breeding father to daughter, half brother to half sister, son to mother, and, by the closest inbreeding of all, brother to sister, stability and purity of inherited material is obtained. Specifically, inbreeding concentrates both good features and faults, strengthening dominants and bringing recessives out into the open where they can be seen and evaluated. It supplies the breeder with the only control he can have over prepotency and homozygosity, or the combining and balancing of similar genetic factors. Inbreeding does not produce degeneration, it merely concentrates weaknesses already present so that they can be recognized and eliminated. This applies to both physical and psychical hereditary transmission.

The most important phases of inbreeding are: (1) To choose as nearly faultless partners as is possible; (2) To cull, or select, rigidly from the resultant progeny.

Selection is always important regardless of which breeding procedure is used, but in inbreeding it becomes imperative. It is of interest to note that the most successful inbreeding programs have used as a base an animal which was either inbred or line-bred. To the breeder, the inbred animal represents an individual whose breeding formula has been so simplified that certain results can almost always be depended upon.

There are many examples of inbreeding over a period of generations in other animal and plant life. Perhaps the most widely known are the experimental rats bred by Dr. Helen L. King, which are the result of over one hundred generations of direct brother and sister mating. The end result has been bigger, finer rodents than the original pair, and entirely dependable uniformity. Dr. Leon F. Whitney has bred and developed a beautiful strain of tropical fish, *Lebistes reticulatus*, commonly known as "guppies," by consecutive brother to sister breeding for ten generations. Dr. Whitney found that each succeeding generation was a little smaller and less vigorous, but that in the fifth generation a change occurred for the better, and in each generation thereafter size, vigor, and color improved.

A very interesting area in genetic research is *heterosis*, or hybrid vigor. The results obtained by this method of breeding in swine, chickens, etc., have been phenomenal. Briefly the basis of *heterosis* is the breeding together of selected brothers and sisters, for many generations to establish strains that are as homozygous (all gene pairs alike) as possible. Through selection, the line is kept going even though the animals (or vegetables) become smaller and less thrifty. After several generations improvements in the intensely inbred lines occur, as though all that was detrimental to the stock has been squeezed out by the intense inbreeding. After the eighth generation two of the lines are crossed. The results obtained in the fields where this breeding has been used are completely heterozygous young (all gene pairs opposite or unalike), with size, vigor, fertility, etc. greater than that of the original pairs with which the breeding was begun. It is doubtful that this type of breeding would be practical in a field such as dog breeding where intelligence, character, and temperament are necessary facets of the breeding picture. It would also be an expensive undertaking to keep two or more lines progressing of direct brother and sister inbreedings; to cull and destroy, always keeping the best pair as breeding partners for the next generation. Lethal faults, hitherto unsuspected in the stock, might become so drastically concentrated as to bring the experiment to a premature conclusion, even if one had the time, money, and energy to attempt it. But such is the inherent character of germ plasm that one direct outcross will tend to bring complete normality to an inbred line drastically weakened by its own concentrated faults.

Helmanhof's Cadenza, owned by Annette Samuels, and bred by Mrs. Helms Crutchfield. Sire: Ch. Helmanhof's Storm Cloud, U.D.; dam: Wave of Mortgaged Acres. Photo by owner.

American fanciers have achieved a high level of success in the breeding of fine Weimaraners. This is largely due to the efforts of astute breeders importing the best available stock' and breeding these dogs wisely until they developed the fine well-balanced dogs seen in the field and on the bench today.

It is essential that the breeder have a complete understanding of the merits of inbreeding, for by employing it skillfully results can be obtained to equal those found in other animal-breeding fields. We must remember that inbreeding in itself creates neither faults nor virtues, it merely strengthens and fixes them in the resulting animals. If the basic stock used is generally good, possessing but few, and those minor, faults, then inbreeding will concentrate all those virtues which are so valuable in that basic stock. Inbreeding gives us great breeding worth by its unique ability to produce prepotency and unusual similarity of type. It exposes the "skeletons in the closet" by bringing to light hitherto hidden faults, so that they may be selected against. We do not correct faults by inbreeding, therefore, we merely make them recognizable so they can be eliminated. The end result of inbreeding, coupled with rigid selection, is complete stability of the breeding material.

Ch. Flott von Haimberg, R.D. (imported), owned by Mr. and Mrs. Adolph Hausserman and bred by Fritz Kuellmer. Sire: Casar von Reiningen; dam: Anka von Bruckberg. Flott, a top sire, is shown winning third in the sporting group at the Devon Dog Show Assoc. under judge William Kendrick, handler Fritz Mueller. Photo by Evelyn Shafer.

Ch. Grave's Rogue, owned and handled by Eldon McCormack, and bred by Raymond M. Graves. Sire Ch. Catalano's Burt; dam: Ch. Graves' Princess von Auger. The judge in this win is Maurice Baker. Photo by Roberts.

With certain strains inbreeding can be capricious, revealing organic weaknesses never suspected that result in decreased vitality, abnormalities—physical and mental—or lethal or crippling factors. Unfortunately, it is not possible to foretell results when embarking on such a program, even if seemingly robust and healthy breeding partners are used as a base. The best chance of success generally comes from the employment of animals which themselves have been strongly inbred and have not been appreciably weakened by it in any way.

An interesting development frequently found in inbreeding is in the extremes produced. The average progeny from inbreeding is equal to the average from line-breeding or outbreeding, but the extremes are greater than those produced by either of the latter breeding methods. Inbreeding, then, is at once capable of producing the best and the worst, and these degrees can be found present in the same litter.

Here again, in inbreeding, as in most of the elements of animal husbandry, we must avoid thinking in terms of human equations. Whether for good or ill, your Weimaraner was man-made, and his destiny and that of his progeny lie in your hands. By selection you improve the strain, culling and killing misfits and monsters. Mankind indulges in no such practice of purification of the race. He mates without any great mental calculation or plan for the future generation. His choice of a mate is both geographically and socially limited in scope. No one plans this mating of his for the future betterment of the breed. Instead, he is blindly led by emotions labeled "love," and sometimes by lesser romantics, "desire." Perish the thought that we should cast

Ch. Strawbridge Oliver, owned by Mr. G. V. Webb (England). Photo by C. M. Cooke and Son.

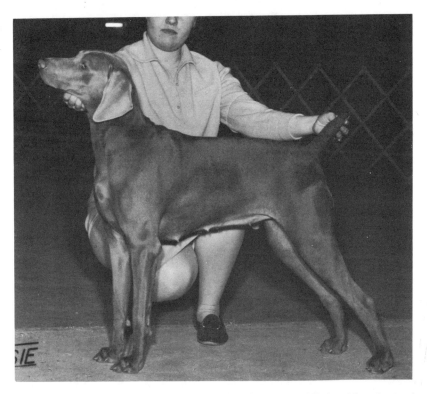

Ch. Tom's Anna Von Verbrandt, owned by Thomas and Esther Versele, and bred by Don and Laura Meyers. Sire: Ch. North Star's Comet; dam: Don's Cinder Aus Der Grau. Photo by Frasie.

mud upon the scented waters of romance, but for our Weimaraners we want something vastly better than the hit-and-miss proposition that has been the racial procedure of man.

Another type of inbreeding, which is not practiced as much as it should be, is "backcrossing." Here we think largely in terms of the male dog, since the element of time is involved. The process involves finding a superior breeding male who is so magnificent in type that we want to perpetuate his qualities and produce, as closely as we can, the prototype of this certain individual. This good male is bred to a fine bitch, and the best female puppy who is similar to her sire in type is bred back again to her sire. Again, the best female puppy is selected and bred back to her sire. This is continued as long as the male can reproduce, or until weaknesses become apparent (if they do) that makes it impractical to continue. If this excellent male seems to have acquired his superiority through the genetic influence of his mother, the first breeding made should possibly be the mating of son to mother, and

Breeders of Weimaraners have achieved the happy harmony of showy dogs that can hunt. Intelligent use of genetic principles have made this desirable situation a reality. Photo by Bill Kohrumel.

the subsequent breedings as described above. In each litter the bitch retained to backcross to her sire should, of course, greatly mirror the sire's type.

LINE-BREEDING

Line-breeding is a broader kind of inbreeding that conserves valuable characteristics by concentration and in a general sense gives us some control of type but a lesser control over specific characteristics. It creates "strains," or "families," within the breed which are easily recognized by their similar conformation. This is the breeding method used by most of the larger kennels, with varied success, since it is not extreme and therefore relatively safe. It is also the method the neophyte is generally advised to employ, for the same reasons.

Specifically, line-breeding entails the selection of breeding partners who have, in their pedigrees, one or more common ancestors. These individuals (or individual) occur repeatedly within the first four or five generations, so that it can be assumed their genetic influence molds the type of succeeding generations. It is a fact that in many breeds success has been obtained by line-breeding to outstanding individuals.

The method varies greatly in intensity, so that some dogs may be strongly line-bred, while others only remotely so. Selection is an important factor here, too, for if we line-breed to procure the specific type of a certain fine animal, then we must select in succeeding generations breeding stock which is the prototype of that individual, or our reason for line-breeding is lost.

One of the chief dangers of line-breeding can be contributed by the breeder of the strain. Many times the breeder reaches a point where he selects his breeding partners on pedigree alone, instead of by individual selection and pedigree combined, within the line.

Crook 'N' Nanny's Flora Dora and Crook 'N' Nanny's Merry Widow, owned and bred by Marie Seidelman, and handled by Rich Milke. Sire: Ch. Gourmet's Theron; dam: Ch. Crook 'N' Nanny's Silver Diana. Photo by Ritter.

In some instances intense line-breeding, particularly when the individual line-bred to is known to be prepotent, can have all the strength of direct inbreeding.

To found a strain which has definite characteristics, within the breed, the following recommendations, based mainly on the work of Humphrey and Warner, and Kelley and Whitney, can be used as a guide.

1. Decide what few traits are essential and what faults are intolerable. Vigor, fertility, character, and temperament must be included in these essentials.

2. Develop a scoring system and score selected virtues and faults in accordance with your breeding aim. Particular stress should be put upon scoring for individual traits which need improvement.

3. Line-breed consistently to the best individuals produced which, by the progeny test show that they will further improve the strain. Inbreeding can be indulged in if the animal used is of exceptional quality and with no outstanding faults. Outcrossings can be made to bring in wanted characteristics if they are missing from the basic stock. Relationship need not be close in the foundation animals, since wide outcrosses will give greater variation and therefore offer a much wider selection of desirable trait combinations.

Every Weimaraner used in this breeding program to establish a strain must be rigidly assessed for individual and breeding excellence and the average excellence of its relatives and its progeny.

Wave of Mortgaged Acres, C.D.X. and Ch. Helmanhof's Storm Cloud, U.D., owned by Mrs. Helms Crutchfield, relax among some of their winnings in the breed and obedience rings. Photo by Annette Samuels.

Ch. Alto von Luddendorff, owned by Ralph and Louise Tennant. Sire: Verdemar's Attila; dam: Ch. Verdemar's Banka. Alto is shown scoring a win under judge Richard L. Fried, handler Walt Shallenbarger. Photo by Bennett.

OUTCROSS BREEDING

Outcross breeding is the choosing of breeding partners whose pedigrees, in the first five or six generations, are free from any common ancestry. With our Weimaraners we cannot outcross in the true sense of the term, since the genetic basis of all Weimaraners, both here and abroad, is based upon the germ plasm of a few selected individuals. To outcross completely, using the term literally (complete heterozygosity), it would be necessary to use an individual of an alien breed as one of the breeding partners.

For the breeder to exercise any control over the progeny of an outcross mating, one of the partners should be inbred or closely line-bred. The other partner should show, in himself and by the progeny test when bred to other bitches, that he is dominant in the needed compensations which are the reasons for the outcross. Thus, by outcross breeding, we bring new and needed characteristics into a strain, along with greater vigor and, generally, a lack of uniformity in the young. Greater uniformity can be achieved if the outcross is made between animals of similar family type. Here again we have a breeding method which has produced excellent individuals, since it tends to conceal recessive genes and promote individual merit. But it generally

Ch. Ring Commander, owned by Mrs. H. B. Barnett, is an example of the excellent type the breeder strives to obtain.

Ch. Bruno von Richard, owned and handled by Walter A. Viebrock, and bred by Richard H. Rance. Sire: Ch. Ann's Ricky Boy, C.D.; dam: Ch. Lady Bran. Bruno is shown going best of winners, under judge Gerhard Plaga. Photo by Norton of Kent.

leads to a lower breeding worth in the outbred animal by dispersing favorable genetic combinations which have given us strain uniformity.

Outcross breeding can be likened to a jigsaw puzzle. We have a puzzle made up of pieces of various shapes and sizes which, when fitted together form a certain pattern. This basic puzzle is comparable to our line-bred or inbred strain. But in this puzzle there are a few pieces that we would like to change, and in so doing change the finished puzzle pattern for the better. By outcrossing we remove some of the pieces and reshape them to our fancy, remembering that these new shapes also affect the shapes of the adjoining pieces, which must then be slightly altered for perfect fit. When this has been successfully accomplished, the finished pattern has been altered to suit our pleasure—we hope.

It sometimes happens that a line-bred or inbred bitch will be outcross-bred to a stud possessed of an open pedigree. It would be assumed by the breeder that the bitch's family type would dominate in the resulting progeny. But occasionally the stud proves himself to be strongly prepotent, and the young instead reflect his individual qualities, not those of the bitch. This can be

Duskin's Princess Shellie, C.D.X., owned by Mr. and Mrs. (handling) Louis A. Pardo and bred by C. J. Russel. Sire: Prince Joe; dam: Russell's Hiedi Ho Silver. Princess Shellie has done equally well in breed and obedience competition, and is handled by her owner in both. Photo by Bennett Associates.

good or bad, depending on what you are looking for in the resultant litter.

Incidentally, when we speak of corrective, or compensation, breeding, we do not mean the breeding of extremes to achieve an intermediate effect. We would not breed an extremely small bitch to an oversized or very large stud in the hope of getting progeny of medium size. The offspring of such a mating would show the size faults of both the extremes. Corrective, or compensation, breeding means the breeding of one partner which is lacking, or faulty, in any specific respect, to an animal which is normal or excellent in the particular area where the other partner is found lacking. In the resulting progeny we can expect to find some young which show the desired improvement.

Ch. Elge of Belle Creek, owned and handled by George Burmeister. Elge is shown finishing to his Canadian championship at the Windsor and District Kennel Club show.

To sum up briefly, we find that *inbreeding* brings us a fixity of type and simplifies the breeding formula. It strengthens desirable dominants and brings hidden and undesirable recessives to the surface where they can be recognized and possibly corrected by *outcross breeding*. When we have thus established definite improvement in type by rigid selection for wanted characteristics, we *line-breed* to create and establish a strain or family line, which in various degrees, incorporates and produces the improvements which have been attained.

In this maze of hidden and obvious genetic stirring, we must not forget the importance of the concrete essence that stands before us. The breeding partners must be examined as individuals in themselves, apart from the story their pedigrees tell us. For as individuals they have been fashioned by, and are the custodians of, their germ plasm, and mirror this fact in their being. Breedings made from paper study only are akin to human marriages arranged in youth by a third party without consulting the partners: they can be consumated, but have small chance of success.

Ch. Crook 'N' Nanny's Morning Mist, owned by Marie Seidelman, and bred by Jean Budler. Sire: Ch. Heinrich Von Houghton; dam: Duchess Florian Grey. Misty came out of the classes to win best of opposite sex at Ravenna (pictured) under judge B. W. Ziessow, enroute to her championship, handler Rich Milke. Photo by Norton of Kent.

Ch. Elken's Toby, owned and bred by Walter and Jo Cox (handling). Sire: Ch. Elken's Vanguard; dam: Elken's Star Lite. Photo by Paul Strobel.

The importance of a pedigree lies in the knowledge we have of the individual animals involved. A fifteen-generation pedigree means nothing if we know nothing about the dogs mentioned. It is more important to extend your knowledge of three or four generations than to extend the pedigree itself. Of real guidance in breeding is a card-index system. This system should indicate clearly the faults and virtues of every pedigree name for at least three generations, with available information as to dominant and recessive traits and the quality of each animal's progeny. At the moment, such a system is practically impossible to achieve. There is little enough known, genetically, about living animals, and the virtues of dogs that are gone are distorted by time and sentiment. To be truly efficacious, near ancestors, as well as littermates, must also be examined for endowed traits, and percentages in regard to these traits correlated and recorded in the pedigree index. From these indexes, graphs could be plotted which would indicate trends within the breed as a whole. To accomplish this design completely, a geneticist would have to be employed and furnished with absolutely truthful information.

The breeding of fine dogs is not a toy to be played with by children. For some of us it forms a nucleus of living, in the esthetic sense. We who give much of our time, thought, and energy to the production of superior stock are often disgusted and disillusioned by the breeding results of others who merely play at breeding, So often individuals long in the game advise the

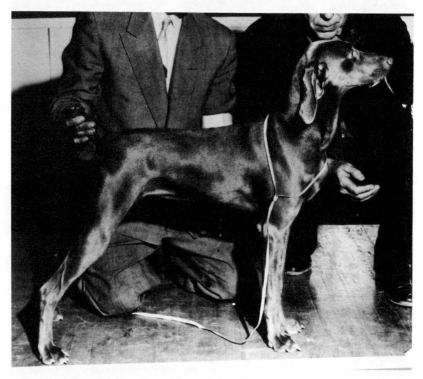

Ch. Crook 'N' Nanny's Silver Diana, owned by Marie Seidelman. Sire: Ch. Alex of Happy Days; dam: Duchess Florian Grey.

novice never to inbreed, but only to line-breed, since in this way the least harm can be done. There has been too much harm done already by novice breeders who should not have been encouraged to breed at all, except under the direct supervision or advice of an experienced or knowledgeable dog man.

The people who compose what we term the Weimaraner "fancy", belong to one of three categories: the novice, the amateur, and the professional.

The novice is one who has recently become enamored of the breed, a tyro, a beginner. Many of them remain in that category indefinitely, due to lack of sincerity or reluctance to learn. Others, eager to absorb all they can, soon rise above the original status.

The professional is one who makes his livelihood from the dog game. His living or employment depends in whole or part upon his kennel activities. A professional must know his business well in order to make it a success, and the earnest professional generally does, though he may occasionally be guilty of breeding for the market.

Numerically, the largest category is that of the amateur. To these individuals the breeding, showing, or training of dogs is a serious hobby. Here are the students of the breed, the people who, in most instances, are well informed, yet avid for new knowledge that will aid in better breeding.

Our novice is many times a charming person who loves his dogs passionately, provides them with more fancy vitamins and supplements than honest food, and treats them with a sloppy sentimentality that even a human baby would resent. He simply can't wait to breed his beautiful bitch and have those appealing puppies. Of course he hasn't the time to acquire a bit of knowledge about the breed, or about the animals in his bitch's pedigree or the stud to which he is going to breed. How then will he have the time or knowledge to care for the pregnant bitch and the subsequent litter properly? Yet inevitably he does find time to listen to the pseudo-professional advice of several self-confessed authorities. In due time this novice is possessed of from seven to ten of the cutest puppies you ever saw, which will in turn be sold to other novices (heaven help them) as show, field and breeding prospects.

By far the greatest menace to the future of the breed is a particular type of wealthy novice. Possessed of the wherewithal to keep and breed any number of dogs, and kennelmen to take care of them, this novice blunders arrogantly forward by virtue of the authority vested in him by his bankbooks and, unhampered by knowledge, breeds indiscriminately, producing litter upon litter of worthless stock. By the law of averages an occasional animal is produced that could qualify V.G. (very good). In the end this novice generally surprisingly and suddenly blossoms out as a full-blown "authority" and judge.

What has been written above is not to be construed as a sweeping condemnation of all novices. Without a constant influx of neophyte breeders, the breed would not be in the high place it is today. Many so-called novices bring to their new breed interest a vast store of canine knowledge collected by an inquiring mind and contact with other breeds.

To repeat, the novice is generally advised by the old-time breeder to begin his new hobby with a line-bred bitch, as this is the cautious approach which leaves the least margin for error. But what of that novice who is essentially what we call a born "dog man"? That individual who, for lack of better

Alf von Forsthaus Dieberg (left) and Nora von Haimberg, GERMAN
Weimaraners, bred by Wilhelm Emmerich and Fritz Kullmer, respectively.
They are owned by and shown with Johan Carlquist of Madrid, Spain.
da Silva Photo.

definition, we say has a "feel" for dogs, who seems to possess an added sense where dogs are concerned?

If this person has an inquiring mind, normal intelligence, and has been associated with other breeds, then the picture of him as the true novice changes. The old-timer will find many times that this "novice" frequently possesses information that the old-timer did not even know existed. This is especially true if the tyro has been exposed to some scientific learning in fields relative to animal advancement. Even experience, which is the old-timer's last-ditch stand, is negligible, for this knowledgeable "novice" can disregard the vagaries of experience with foreknowledge of expectancy.

In most instances this type of novice doesn't begin to think of breeding, of even owning, a specimen of the breed until he has made a thorough study of background, faults, virtues, and genetic characters. To him, imitation is not a prelude to success. Therefore, the line-bred bitch, modeled by another's ego, is not for him. The outcross bitch, whose genetic composition presents a challenge and which, by diligent study and application of acquired knowledge, can become the fountainhead of a strain of his own, is the answer to his need.

Some of what you have read here in reference to the novice may have seemed to be cruel caricature. Actually, it is not caricature, but it is cruel and meant to stress a point. We realize that to some novices our deep absorption in all the many aspects of breed betterment may seem silly or ridiculous. But the genetic repercussion of breeding stupidity can echo down through generations, making a mockery of our own intense, sometimes heartbreaking, and often humble, striving toward an ideal.

Chapter V
Feeding

Your Weimaraner is a carnivore, a flesh eater. His teeth are not made for grinding as are human teeth, but are chiefly fashioned for tearing and severing. Over a period of years this fact has led to the erroneous conclusion that the dog must be fed mostly on muscle meat in order to prosper. Wolves, jackals, wild dogs, and foxes comprise the family Canidae to which your dog belongs. These wild relatives of the dog stalk and run down their living food in the same manner the dog would employ if he had not become attached to man. The main prey of these predators are the various hoofed herbivorous animals, small mammals and birds of their native habitat. The carnivores consume the entire body of their prey, not just the muscle meat alone.

You would assume, and rightly so, that the diet which keeps these wild cousins of the dog strong, healthy, and fertile could be depended upon to do

Proper food and the right amounts of it are absolutely necessary to the growth and development of a breed as large and active as the Weimaraner. Photo by Louise Van der Meid.

Anyone who breeds Weimaraners should be aware that the best invest-
ments in food and feeding always repay themselves in the vigor and tone
of the animals in one's breeding stock. Photo by Annette Samuels.

Sound feeding practices always begin with the brood bitch. A well-nourished bitch can usually be depended upon to produce a litter of good, sturdy puppies.

the same for your Weimaraner. Of course, in this day and age your dog cannot live off the land. He depends upon you for sustenance, and to feed him properly, you must understand what essential food values the wild carnivore derives from his kill, for this is nature's supreme lesson in nutrition.

The canine hunter first laps the blood of his victim, then tears open the stomach and eats its contents, composed of predigested vegetable matter. He feasts on liver, heart, kidneys, lungs, and the fat-encrusted intestines. He crushes and consumes the bones and the marrow they contain, feeds on fatty meat and connective tissue, and finally eats the lean muscle meat. From the blood, bones, marrow, internal organs, and muscle meat he has absorbed minerals and proteins. The stomach and its contents have supplied vitamins and carbohydrates. From the intestines and fatty meat he gets fats, fatty acids, vitamins, and carbohydrates. Other proteins come from the ligaments and connective tissue. Hair and some indigestible parts of the intestinal contents provide enough roughage for proper laxation. From the action of the sun and from the water he drinks, he is provided with supplementary vitamins

Ch. Von Agar's Wachtell, C.D., owned by Captain Hoyt (England). Photo by C. M. Cooke and Son.

and minerals. From his kill, therefore, the carnivore acquires a well-rounded diet. To supply these same essentials to your dog in a form which you can easily purchase is the answer to his dietary needs.

BASIC FOODS AND SUPPLEMENTS

From the standpoint of nutrition, any substance may be considered food which can be used by an animal as a body-building material, a source of energy, or a regulator of body activity. From the preceding paragraphs we have learned that muscle meat alone will not fill these needs and that your Weimaraner's diet must be composed of many other food materials to provide elements necessary to his growth and health. These necessary ingredients can be found in any grocery store. There you can buy all the important natural sources of the dietary essentials listed below.

1. PROTEIN: meat, dairy products, eggs, soybeans.
2. FAT: butter, cream, oils, fatty meat, milk, cream, cheese, suet.
3. CARBOHYDRATES: cereals, vegetables, confectionery syrups, honey.
4. VITAMIN A: greens, peas, beans, asparagus, broccoli, eggs, milk.
5. THIAMINE: vegetables, legumes, whole grains, eggs, muscle meats, organ meats, milk, yeast.

Water is essential to all life. Weimaraner puppies should be allowed a constant supply, which should always be fresh and cool. Photo by Louise Van der Meid.

Ch. Wetobe's Blue Bing, C.D., owned, bred and handled by Mrs. H. B. Barnett. Sire: Ch. Casar's Bing; dam: Wetobe's Silver Lady. Bing is seen going winners at the Weimaraner Club of Louisiana, under judge Virgil Johnson. Photo by Alexander.

6. RIBOFLAVIN: green leaves, milk, liver, cottonseed flour or meal, egg yolk, wheat germ, yeast, beef, chicken.
7. NIACIN: milk, lean meats, liver, yeast.
8. VITAMIN D: fish that contains oil (salmon, sardine, herring, cod), fish liver oils, eggs, fortified milk.
9. ASCORBIC ACID: tomatoes, citrus fruits, raw cabbage (it has not been established that ascorbic acid is necessary for dogs).
10. IRON, CALCIUM, AND PHOSPHORUS: milk and milk products, vegetables, eggs, soybeans, bone marrow, blood, liver, oatmeal.

The first three listed essentials complement each other and compose the basic nutritional needs. Proteins build new body tissue and are composed of amino acids, which differ in combination with the different proteins. Carbohydrates furnish the fuel for growth and energy, and fat produces heat which becomes energy and enables the dog to store energy against emergency. Vitamins and minerals, in general, act as regulators of cell activity.

Proteins are essentially the basis of life, for living cells are composed of protein molecules. In this connection, an interesting scientific experiment was conducted a short while ago which led to an important discovery. A young scientist attempted to duplicate the conditions which, it is assumed, prevailed upon the earth before life began. Cosmological theory indicates that the atmosphere at that time (approximately two thousand million years ago, give or take a year) would have been poisonous to all the living organisms that exist today, with the exception of certain bacteria. When the experiment had been completed, it was found that amino acids had formed. These chemicals are the building blocks of proteins, and proteins are the basis of life. No, science has not yet produced actual life by building proteins. It is still rather difficult to even define life, let alone manufacture it. But we can sustain and give growth to living forms by proper feeding procedures.

The main objective in combining food factors is to mix them in the various amounts necessary to procure a balanced diet. This can be done in a number of ways. The essential difference in the many good methods of feeding lies in the time it takes to prepare the food and in the end cost of the materials used. Dogs can be fed expensively and they can be fed cheaply, and in each instance they can be fed equally well.

Dogs look to their owners for every one of their life requirements. It is the duty of the dog owner to meet these needs at all times. Photo by Annette Samuels.

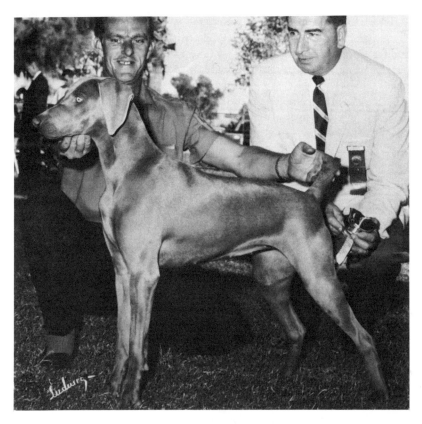

Ch. Smoky's Kate Smith, owned by Darrel D. Engenauer, and bred by H. L. and Mary B. Robinson. Sire Ch. Bando v.d. Gretchenhof; dam: Ch. Smoky Heritage. She is being handled to a four point major enroute to her championship under judge Robert Waters, handler Lee Wenrich. Photo by Joan Ludwig.

There are various food products on the market packaged specifically for canine consumption. The quality of these foods as complete diets in themselves ranges from poor to excellent. The better *canned* foods are good but expensive for large breeds such as ours, since the moisture content is high and your Weimaraner must consume a large amount for adequate nourishment. Compact and requiring no preparation, the canned foods are fine for use at shows or when traveling, though for traveling an even better diet is biscuits, lean meat, and very little water. The result is less urination and defecation, since the residue from this diet is very small. The diet is, of course, not to be fed over any extended period of time because it lacks food-value.

Biscuits can be considered as tidbits rather than food, since much of the vitamin and mineral content has been destroyed by baking. The same holds true for *kibbled* or "broken-biscuit" foods. They are fillers to which must be added, fat, milk, broths, meat, vegetables, and vitamin and mineral supplement.

By far the most complete of the manufactured foods are the *grain foods*. In such a highly competitive business as the manufacturing and merchandising of these foods, it is essential for the manufacturer to market a highly palatable and balanced ration. The better grain foods have constantly changing formulas to conform to the most recent results of scientific dietary research. They are, in many cases, the direct result of controlled generation tests in scientific kennels where their efficacy can be ascertained. A good grain food should not be considered merely a filler. Rather, it should be employed as the basic diet to which fillers might possibly be added. Since the grain food is bag or box packaged and not hermetically sealed, the fat content is necessarily low. A high degree of fat would produce quick rancidity. Therefore fat must be added to the dry food. Milk, which is one of the finest of foods in itself, can be added along with broths or plain warm water to arrive at the proper consistency for palatability. With such a diet we have a true balance of essentials, wastage is kept to a minimum, stools are small and firm and easily removed, and cost and labor have been reduced to the smallest equation possible to arrive at and yet feed well. The *pellet type* food, often referred to as kibble, is simply grain food to which a binding agent has been added to hold the grains together in the desired compact form.

Fat should be introduced into the dog's diet in its pure form. Proteins and carbohydrates are converted into fat by the body. Fat also causes the dog to retain his food longer in the stomach. It stores vitamins A, D, E, and K, and lessens the bulk necessary to be fed at each meal. Fat can be melted and poured over the meal, or put through the meat grinder and then mixed with the basic ration.

Just as selection is important in breeding, so ratio is important in feeding. The proper diet must not only provide all the essentials, it must also supply those essentials in the proper proportions. This is what we mean by a balanced diet. It can be dangerous to your dog's well being if the ratios of any of his dietary essentials are badly unbalanced over a period of time. The effects can be disastrous in the case of puppies. This is the basic reason for putting your faith in a good, scientifically balanced grain dog food.

There is an abundance of concentrated *vitamin supplements* on the market specifically manufactured for dogs. They are of real worth if your dog needs a supplement. Dogs fed a balanced diet, however, do not need additional concentrated supplements, with the exception, perhaps, of the rare individual. If you feel that your dog is in need of a supplement, it is wiser to consult

Jan's Radar, owned by W. S. and Agnes M. Tomerlin, and bred by W. S. Tomerlin. Sire: F. T. Ch. Ludwig von Weisenhof; dam: Ch. Leer's Jan Tomerlin, S.D.X., R.D.X. Radar is shown going best of winners at the Weimaraner Club of America specialty held with the Harbor Cities Kennel Club. This win was scored in an entry of ninety-seven Weimaraners, under judge Maxwell Riddle. The handler of this fine dog is Robert Kelton. Photo by Bill Francis.

your veterinarian for advice and specific dosage. Check the label of the dog food you buy to make sure that it has all the necessary ingredients. If it has, you will not find it necessary to pour in concentrated, highly expensive supplements. Another of the supplements widely in use today, packaged under various trade names, embodies the elements of what was initially called A.P.F., or animal protein factor. This is a powder combining various antibiotic residues with the composite vitamin B_{12}. The role of this supplement in dog feeding has not, as yet, been adequately established. Theoretically, it is supposed that this supplement produces better food utilization and the production of extra body fat, which accounts for better growth and weight. On the other hand, it is also thought that it can affect the normal balance of intestinal flora, and overdoses can produce undesirable effects. Nature is generally generous in her gift of vitamins, minerals, and other nutritional essentials, and all can be found, in adequate abundance, in the balanced diet. I do not want to rule out supplements, but I do want to stress that they should be used with care.

In many instances kennel owners feel that their animals, for various reasons, need a supplementary boost in their diet. Some are in critical stages

Ch. Holly Austa Fawn, owned and handled by George Burmeister, shown finishing her Canadian championship at Sarnia.

Ch. Elsmere's Baron Von Sturm, owned by Frank and Leona Cascino, and bred by N. Delorio. Sire: Elsmere's King; dam: Elsmere's Missy. Sturm is pictured with his handler, Edward Larsen. Photo by Evelyn Shafer.

of growth, bitches are about to be bred or are in whelp, mature dogs are being frequently used for stud, and others are recuperating from illness. In such cases commercial supplements can be added to the food, but in reasonable amounts, or brewers' yeast, alfalfa meal, and similar natural agents can be mixed separately in a container and judicious quantities added to the basic diet.

Calcium and *phosphorus* in pure chemical form must be handled with care when used in the dog's diet. Toxic conditions can be caused by an overabundance of this material in the bloodstream. Green, ground, edible bone meal is a much better product to use where it is thought necessary. Most good grain foods have an abundance of this inexpensive element in correct balance. Milk is a highly desirable vehicle for balanced calcium and phosphorus as well as many other nutritional needs.

Cod liver oil is another product that, if given to excess over a period of time, can cause toxicity and bone malformation. It is better and cheaper to employ a fish liver oil concentrate such as percomorph oil. In this oil the base vehicle has been discarded and the pure oil concentrated, so that a very small dosage is required. Many owners and breeders pour cod liver oil and throw

91

handfuls of calcium and supplementary concentrates into the food pans in such lavish amounts that there is a greater bulk of these than of the basic food, on the theory that, if a little does some good, a greater amount will be of immense benefit. This concept is both ridiculous and dangerous.

An occasional pinch of *bicarbonate of soda* in the food helps to neutralize stomach acidity and can prevent, or alleviate, fatigue caused by a highly acid diet. Bones need never be fed to dogs for food value if the diet is complete. Poultry bones should never be fed. They splinter into sharp shards which can injure gums or rip the throat lining. Once in the stomach they are dissolved by strong gastric juices. It is on their way to their ultimate goal that they do damage. The same is also true of fishbones. If you want to give your Weimaraner something to chew on, get one of the rawhide or nylon bones found in pet shops.

Table scraps are supplements only, and if your dog is a good eater and easy keeper, give him leftovers from time to time in his food pan. The diets of good feeders can be varied to a greater extent without unfavorable repercussions than can the diets of finicky eaters. Fish is a good food, containing all the food elements which are found in meat, with a bonus of extra nutritional values. *Muscle meat* lacks many essentials and is so low in calcium that, even when supplemented with vitamin D, there is grave danger of rickets developing. In its raw state, meat is frequently the intermediate host

Alarcon von den Weberhof (left) and Abbie von den Weberhof, owned by Johan Carlquist and bred by Ellen Carlquist Weber. Photo by da Silva.

Ch. Gronbach's Aladdin, C.D., owned, bred and handled by Robert C. Gronbach. Sire: Ch. Durmar's Karl; dam: Ch. Norman's Nifty Nina. This handsome dog is shown winning the sporting group at the Walkill Kennel Club under judge C. Y. Smith. Among his many fine wins, Aladdin was the winner of the sporting group at the Westminster Kennel Club, 1965. Photo by Evelyn Shafer.

of several forms of internal parasites. Meat by-products and canned meat, which generally contains by-products, are much better as food for dogs than pure muscle meat. Incidentally, whale meat, which is over eighty percent protein, could well replace horse meat, which is less than fifty percent protein, in the dog's diet.

Water is one of the elementary essentials. Considering the fact that the dog's body is approximately seventy percent water, which is distributed in varying percentages throughout the body tissues and organs, including the teeth and bones, it isn't difficult to realize the importance of this staple to the dog's well being. Water flushes the system, stimulates gastric juice activity, brings about better appetite, and acts as a solvent within the body. It is one of the major sources of necessary minerals and helps during hot weather, and to a lesser degree during winter, to regulate the dog's temperature. When a dog is kept from water for any appreciable length of time, dehydration occurs. This is a serious condition, a fact which is known to any dog owner whose animal has been affected by diarrhea, continuous nausea, or any of the diseases in which this form of body shrinkage occurs.

Ch. Gretchenhof Jolly Roger, owned by Ralph and Louise Tennant. Sire: Ch. Hilltop's Mistifritz; dam: Ch. Cilly v.d. Gretchenhof. This top winning western campaigner is shown with his handler, Walt Shallenbarger. Photo by Joan Ludwig.

Ch. Smoky's Snap-Shot, owned by M. M. and Louise Brown, and bred by Mary Robinson. Sire: Ch. Bando v.d. Gretchenhof; dam: Ch. Smoky Heritage. Photo by Joan Ludwig.

Sh. Ch. Wolfox Silver Glance, owned by Mrs. B. Douglas-Redding (England). Photo by C. M. Cooke and Son.

Water is the cheapest part of your dog's diet, so supply it freely, particularly in warm weather. In winter if snow and ice are present and available to your Weimaraner, water is not so essential. At any rate, if left in a bucket in his run, it quickly turns to ice. Yet even under these conditions it is an easy matter to bring your dog in and supply him with at least one good drink of fresh water during the day. Being so easily provided, so inexpensive, and so highly essential to your Weimaraner's health, sober thought dictates that we should allow our dogs to "take to drink."

Breeders with only a few dogs can sometimes afford the extra time, expense, and care necessary to feed a varied and complicated diet. But it is easy to see that to feed a large kennel in such fashion would take an immense amount of time, labor, and expense. Actually, the feeding of a scientifically balanced grain food as the basic diet eliminates the element of chance which exists in diets prepared by the kennel owner from natural sources, since overabundance of some specific elements, as well as a lack of others, can bring about dietary ills and deficiencies.

Caloric requirements vary with age, temperament, changes in temperature, and activity. If your dog is nervous, very active, young, and kept out of doors in winter, his caloric intake must be greater than the phlegmatic, underactive, fully grown dog who has his bed in the house. Keep your Weimaraner in good flesh, neither too fat nor too thin. You are best judge of the amount to feed him to keep him in his best condition. A well-fed Weimaraner should always be in show "bloom": clear-eyed, glossy-coated, filled with vim and vigor, and with enough of an all-over layer of fat to give him sleekness without plumpness.

FEEDING TECHNIQUES

The consistency of the food mix can vary according to your Weimaraner's taste. It is best not to serve the food in too sloppy a mixture, except in the case of very young puppies. It is also good practice to feed the same basic

Sh. Ch. Theocsbury Abbie, owned by Mrs. S. M. Roberts. (England). Photo by C. M. Cooke and Son.

Ch. Aurora v. Graff, owned by Richard P. Graff, and bred by Walter Trevaskis. Sire: Nurmi vom Haimberg (Imp.); dam: Pi Ply-Weimar. This nicely balanced bitch is shown winning best of breed at the Talbot Kennel Club under judge William L. Kendrick, handler Peggy Kepler Rousch. Photo by Evelyn Shafer.

ration at every meal so that the taste of the food does not vary greatly at each feeding. Constant changing of the diet, with supplementary meals of raw or cooked meat, tends to produce finicky eaters, the bane of the kennel and private owner's existence. Never leave the food pan before your Weimaraner for more than thirty minutes. If he hasn't eaten by then, or has merely nibbled, the pan should be removed and not presented to him again until his next feeding time. This same policy should be followed when breaking a dog to a new diet. If he has become a canine gourmet, spoiled by a delicate diet, he may sometimes refuse to eat for two or three days. But eventually, when his hunger becomes acute enough and he realizes his hunger strike will not result in coddling and the bringing forth of his former delicacies, he will eat with gusto whatever is put before him. Remember, your Weimaraner is not a lap dog; he is a big and powerful hunting dog and should not be babied. Where there are several dogs to create mealtime competition, there is little danger of finicky eaters regardless of what is fed.

Keep your feeding utensils clean to eliminate the danger of bacterial formation and sourness, especially in warm weather. Your food pans can be of any solid metal material. Agate, porcelain, and the various types of enamelware have a tendency to chip, and are therefore not desirable.

Every kennel owner and breeder has his own pet diet which has proven successful in the rearing and maintenance of his stock. In each instance he will insist that his is the only worth-while diet, and he cannot be blamed for so asserting, since his particular diet has nourished and kept his own stock in top condition over a period of years. Yet the truth is, as we have mentioned before in this chapter, that there are many ways to feed dogs and feed them well, and no one diet can be said to be the best.

Perhaps it would be enlightening to the reader to explain how the dogs are fed in two fairly small kennels, as well as the feeding procedure used in a much larger kennel. The results of these three different diets have all been excellent. There have been no runts, the growth factor in each instance has been entirely adequate, and none of the animals bred or raised have shown any signs of nutritional lack. All the dogs raised on these diets have developed normally into the full flower of their genetic inheritance, with lustrous coats, fine teeth and bones, and all possessing great vigor and stamina. Incidentally, what has previously been written in this chapter is applicable mostly to grown dogs, though the three feeding formulas to follow include puppy feeding as well. A more comprehensive study of puppy feeding will be found in the chapter dealing specifically with puppies.

Diet Number 1

Dietol, an oil product, is given the puppies in the nest on the second day after whelping; two drops to each puppy. The amount is gradually increased, until the second week each puppy is receiving ten drops of the oil. The third week, twenty drops are given, and this is continued until a full pint has been consumed.

At twelve to fourteen days, for a litter of six puppies, a cereal is cooked with one-eighth of a pound of butter or margarine, or a good special puppy meal is substituted for the cereal. To this is added one-half a can of evaporated milk, two poached eggs, cow's milk, and two tablespoonfuls of Karo syrup. This is fed twice daily to supplement the dam's feedings.

At three weeks, the same diet is given three times a day.

At four weeks, the same diet, given four times a day. At this time, chopped beef, rich in fat, is added, and two eggs are cooked in with the cereal.

Between the fifth and sixth weeks the puppies are weaned. During this period, two feedings are the same as the diet fed during the fourth week, and two other feedings are composed of a good grain dog meal, moistened

Sh. Ch. Wolfox Lycidas, owned by Mrs. B. Douglas-Redding (England). Photo by C. M. Cooke and Son.

Ch. Miss BB von Zwei Vogel, owned by Mr. and Mrs. Richard L. Byrd, and bred by William E. Ashby and Thomas L. Byrd. Sire: Traveler v.d. Drei Brunnen; dam: Zelda von Franzen. She is shown winning best of breed at the Imperial Valley Kennel Club under judge Frank Porter Miller, handler, Robert Kelton. Photo by Bennett Associates.

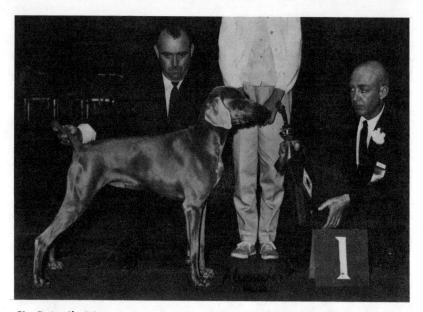

Ch. Dzigel's Silver Joy, owned by Miss Renee Loyless, and bred by John F. and Glenda Sigel. Sire: Ch. Angelo's Sure Shot Skeet; dam: Ch. Dzigel's Gay Lady, C.D. Joy is shown winning the sporting group at the Galveston County Kennel Club under judge Langdon Skarda, handler Harold Bishop. Photo by Alexander.

with broth or soup, to which has been added a heaping handful of chopped beef which is at least twenty-five percent fat. This food mixture is supplemented by three tablespoons of refined cod liver oil and a heaping tablespoon of a mixture of bone meal, soybean meal, brewer's yeast, and a small amount of salt.

Three meals are fed as described above at three months and continued until the puppies have reached the age of five months, the only variation being the use of small kibbles occasionally replacing the basic cereal or meal at two of the meals.

From five months until twelve to fourteen months, two large meals are given, one in the morning and one at night, using the same diet as above, augmented by any and all table scraps, from potatoes and sauerkraut to cake.

From fourteen months on the dog is fed once daily in the summer. In fall and winter the diet consists of a light breakfast of warm cereal, milk, and Karo syrup. The main evening meal is composed of grain meal or, occasionally, kibbles or pellets, moistened in soup or warm water, a pound of ground fatty meat, one tablespoonful of cod liver oil or Dietol, and a heaping tablespoon of the mixed supplement mentioned previously (bone meal, soybean

Ch. Kit's Marbarle's Jato, C.D.X., S.D., R.D., owned by Robert D. Bruaw, and bred by Dr. Ernest M. Lerner. Sire: Ch. Treu von Frakker; dam: Kit and Kaboodle, U.D; he is shown winning the breed under Frank Foster Davis, Handler Mrs. Bruaw. Photo by Evelyn Shafer.

meal, and yeast). To this is added table scraps of every description, except fowl bones and fishbones.

During the winter months occasional stews of beef or lamb and fresh vegetables are relished by the dogs.

Diet Number 2

Dietol is given each puppy in increasing amounts as it grows, beginning with two drops for Weimaraner puppies. This oil is rich in vitamin K, which is an essential vitamin for puppy survival.

At sixteen days the pups are given their first supplementary feeding. From then on the Dietol is incorporated in their meals. A puppy grain meal, Pampa, is used as a base, to which is added a tablespoonful of Pelargon, a Nestle's dried milk product which has been enriched and acidified so that it more closely approaches the taste of the bitch's milk than does plain cow's milk. (Incidentally, if you've brought a puppy home who refuses to eat, try this product mixed with warm milk or sprinkled over the food mixture.

Care must be taken in the feeding of developing puppies, that their meals not be cut down abruptly or their food changed suddenly, as this can cause a certain amount of intestinal upset.

Ch. Casar von Richard, owned by Dorothy A. Newsom, and bred by Richard Rance. Sire: Baron von Richard; dam: Ch. Asta von Richard. Casar is being handled to a best of breed win under judge Elbert Vary, by Bennie Dennard. Photo by Alexander.

In almost every instance it will do the trick.) Warmed cow's milk and about ten percent melted fat is added to the Pampa and Pelargon. Stir to the consistency of cream and allow them to eat all they can hold.

At three weeks the same mixture is fed three times a day.

At four weeks, the same mixture is fed four times a day. The fat content is raised to about fifteen percent. The consistency of the food is slightly thickened, and a natural supplement, composed of alfalfa leaf meal, irradiated yeast, and ground bone meal, is added sparingly. The ratios of these ingredients, mixed together in a large jar for continued use are: two tablespoonfuls of alfalfa leaf meal to one tablespoonful of yeast and three-quarters of a tablespoonful of bone meal.

At six weeks the puppies are completely weaned and fed five times daily. Four of the meals are the same mixture as used at four weeks, with a small amount of canned horse meat added for taste and a scent appeal. The meals are increased in size with the growth of the pups. The last meal, the fifth at night, consists of warmed milk, half natural cow and half evaporated. After eight weeks the Pelargon is discontinued and powdered milk is used instead.

Five feedings are given until three months. Four feedings from then up to five months.

From five months until eight months, three feedings are given, eliminating the late evening milk meal. The dog is switched then from Pampa to a regular grain meal (in this instance either Lifespan or Kasco, since both are easily available and are good grain foods). Milk is added to all other meals in powder or liquid form.

Two meals from eight to eighteen months, are fed and thereafter one meal, unless, as is generally the case, the individual thrives better on two meals.

Table scraps of all kinds are used whenever available, exclusive of fowl bones and fishbones. The schedule as outlined above is not necessarily a rigid one. Fish, stews, eggs (yolks only if raw, whole egg if cooked), liver, and a host of other foods are occasionally incorporated into the diet. But this is the one main, day in, day out, diet.

Diet Number 3

This diet is used by Dr. Leon F. Whitney for his Redbone Coonhounds, which are approximately the same size as Weimaraners. During the hunting season they are hunted extensively, running miles and miles of woodland nightly, trailing their quarry. Bitches are bred regularly, whelping large litters of healthy pups.

At sixteen to eighteen days supplementary feeding is begun, consisting of Pampa (or a like product) and warmed evaporated milk. This mixture (of creamy consistency) is fed three times a day.

At seven weeks the puppies are completely weaned and receive four feedings daily as described above. Fat is now added to the diet to the amount of twenty percent of the dry weight of the complete ration.

This amount of fat is incorporated into the diet until the puppies are three to four months of age. At this time the puppies are changed to a tested adult grain meal and the fat incorporated raised to twenty-five percent of the dry total. The puppies are then fed twice daily, with hot water replacing the milk, until fully grown.

With full growth, only one daily feeding is given, consisting of the same diet as above.

Dr. Whitney's kennels houses sixty or more Redbones, as well as a large number of Beagles used in dietary and other experimentation. Breeders with only a few dogs can generally afford the extra time, expense, and care necessary to feed varied and complicated diets, but to feed a kennel of sixty

Ch. Cilly v.d. Gretchenhof, owned by Ralph and Louise Tennant. Sire: Ch. Hans v.d. Gretchenhof, C.D.; dam: Ch. Quicksilver Lady, C.D. This bitch has compiled one of the breed's leading records in her sex, as a show dog and has also demonstrated her worth as a producer of champions. Photo by Joan Ludwig.

dogs on complicated diets would take an immense amount of time and labor, not to mention expense, and is therefore not feasible.

Of course to the ordinary breeder, working with a limited amount of stock, every breeding made is the result of intense study and much discussion, since every breeding made is eminently important and must not be wasted. Then, to complement the results of breeding, a complete and balanced diet is necessary to follow through and bring the resulting get to a correct and healthy maturity.

Remember always that feeding ranks next to breeding in the influence it exerts on the growing dog. Knowledgeable breeding can produce genetically fine specimens, selection can improve the strain and the breed, but, without full and proper nourishment, particularly over the period of growth, the dog cannot attain to the promise of his heritage. The brusque slogan of a famous cattle breeder might well be adopted by breeders of Weimaraners. The motto is, "Breed, feed, weed."

Chapter VI
General Care

When you own a dog, you own a dependent. Though the Internal Revenue Department does not recognize this fact, it is nevertheless true. Whatever pleasure one gets out of life must be paid for in some kind of coin, and this is as applicable to the pleasure we derive from our dogs as it is in all things. With our dogs we pay the toll of constant care. This Weimaraner which you have taken into your home and made a part of your family life depends completely upon you for his every need. In return for the care you give him, he repays you with a special brand of love and devotion that can't be duplicated. That is the bargain you make with your dog: your care on one side of the scale, his complete idolatry on the other. Not quite a fair bargain, but we humans, unlike our dogs, are seldom completely fair and unselfish.

The Weimaraner has found many friends among American dog lovers. For the care he deserves, he returns a full measure of loyalty, devotion and matchless, birdy elegance. Photo by Louise Van der Meid.

Good husbandry pays off in dollars and cents too, particularly if you have more than one or two dogs, or run a semicommercial kennel. Clean, well-cared for dogs are most often healthy dogs, free from parasitic invaders and the small ills that bring other and greater woes in their wake. Good feeding and proper exercise help build strength and resistance to disease, and a sizable run keeps your canine friend from wandering into the path of some speeding car. Veterinarian bills and nursing time are substantially reduced, saving you money and time, when your dog is properly cared for.

Cleanliness, that partner to labor which is owned by some to be next to godliness, is the first essential of good dog care. This applies to the dog's surrounding environment as well as to the dog himself. If your Weimaraner sleeps in the house, provide him with a draft-free spot for his bed, away from general household traffic. This bed can be a piece of rug or a well-padded dog mattress. It doesn't particularly matter what material is used as long as it is kept clean and put in the proper place.

Feeding has been comprehensively discussed in the previous chapter, but the utensils used and the methods of feeding come more specifically under the heading of general care, so we will repeat these few facts mentioned in the previous chapter. Heavy aluminium feeding pans are best, since they are easily cleaned and do not chip as does agate or porcelain. Feed your dog regularly in the same place and at the same time. Establish a friendly and quiet atmosphere during feeding periods and do not coax him to eat. If he

Although the Weimaraner is a relative newcomer to American dogdom, he has caught on quickly as a field and bench dog. This group is typical of the dogs and owners that are bringing the Weimaraner to prominence in the field.

Correct management brings its own rewards in clean healthy stock, vigorous stud dogs, sturdy brood bitches, and large litters of strong puppies. To economize in the care and management of one's stock is truly false economy. Unthrifty animals will result from corner cutting. Photo by Louise Van der Meid.

refuses the food or nibbles at it sparingly, remove his food and do not feed again until the next feeding period. Never allow a pan of food to stand before a healthy dog for more than thirty minutes under any circumstances. Should your Weimaraner's appetite continue to be off, consult your veterinarian for the cause.

If you are feeding several dogs in an outside kennel, it is good practice to remain until all are finished, observing their appetites and eating habits while you wait. Often two dogs, kenneled together and given the same amount and kind of food, show different results. One will appear thin and the other in good condition. Sometimes the reason is a physiological one, but more often observation will show that the thinner dog is a slower eater than his kennel mate; that the latter dog gulps down his own food and then drives the thin dog away from his food pan before his ration is fully consumed and finishes this extra portion, too.

Never, never, force feed a healthy dog simply because he refuses an occasional meal. Force feeding and coaxing make finicky eaters and a finicky feeder is never in good coat or condition and turns feeding time into the most exasperating experience of the day. Rather than forcing or coaxing, it

While the Weimaraner is, by nature, an accomplished hunter, he gets along well with most house pets. Ch. Schmidt's Valiant Knight, owned by William Schmidt, and "Angus McTavish" seem to have an accord. Photo by J. Lewis.

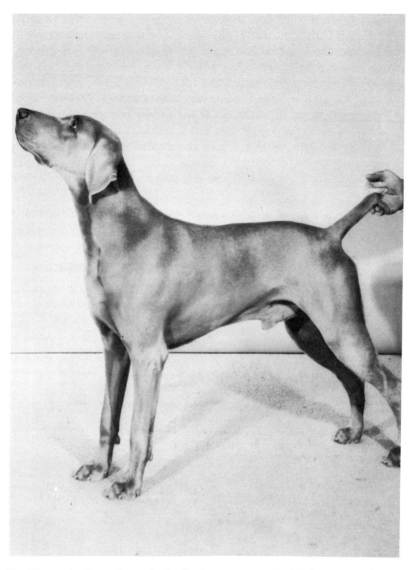

Ch. Viermar's Gettysburg Gallant, C.D., owned by Walter A. Viebrock, and bred by Vivian C. Viebrock and owner. Sire: Ch. Bruno von Richard; dam: Gretchen Von Viebrock. This dog was handled to his bench and obedience titles by his owner-co-breeder. Photo by Engler.

is better to starve your dog, showing no sympathy at all when he refuses food. If he is healthy, he will soon realize that he will experience hunger unless he eats when the food pan is put before him and will soon develop a normal and healthy appetite. Immediately upon removing the food pans, they should be thoroughly washed and stacked, ready for the next mealtime.

During hot weather, be certain that your Weimaraner has a constant supply of fresh, clean water. In winter, water left outside in runs will freeze solid and be of no use to the dogs, so it is best to provide fresh water two or three times a day and remove the pail after the dogs have had their fill. Always provide water within an hour after feeding.

It has been the experience of most dog people that animals kept or ken-

Ch. Helmanhof's Uhlan, C.D.X., owned and bred by Mrs. Helms Crutch-field. Sire: Ch. Helmanhof's Storm Cloud, U.D.; dam: Wave of Mortgaged Acres, C.D.X. Photo by Annette Samuels.

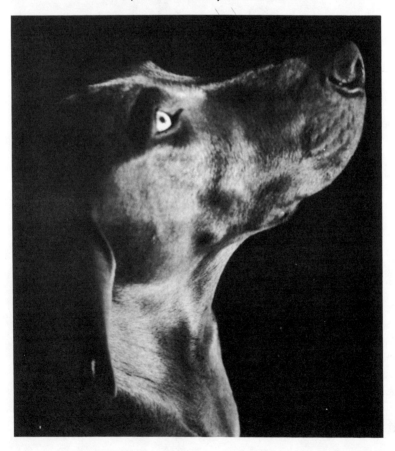

Bongold's Countess Linda Lee, owned by L. C. Hanna. She is shown winning best of opposite sex at the Kennel Club of Virginia, pictured with her handler, Tom Gately. Photo by Annette Samuels.

neled outdoors, both winter and summer, are healthier and in better condition generally than their softer-living housedog brethren. Light and the seasons have a great deal to do with shedding and coat condition. The outdoor dog, living in an environment approaching the natural, has regular shedding periods, after which his new coat comes in hard, strong, and glossy. Housedogs living in conditions of artificial light and heat seem to shed constantly, and seldom possess the good coat exhibited by the Weimaraner who lives outdoors. The housedog is much more susceptible to quick changes in temperature, particularly in the winter when he is brought from a warm, furnace-heated house, into the frigid out-of-doors. Never forget that your Weimaraner is a strong and powerful hunting dog, not a lap dog, and treat him accordingly. Babying an individual of a breed of such high intelligence can produce a nuisance or a canine hypochondriac.

PLANNING YOUR RUN

Even the housedog should be provided with an outside run and house, a domain of his own to keep him in the sun and air and protect him from disturbance by children or other dogs. There, in his run, he is safe from accident, and you know he can't run away to become lost, strayed, or stolen. There, also, you can be sure he is not soiling or digging in your neighbor's newly planted lawn, a situation which can strain, to put it mildly, any "good-neighbor policy." Provide shade in some section of the run against the hot summer sun. Natural shade from trees is the ideal, of course, but artificial shade can be provided by a canvas overthrow placed strategically.

The run should be as large as your property will permit. Twenty by forty feet is a good size for one or two dogs, but if space permits it, a longer run is preferable. If you are building, a kennel of several runs, remember that the length is more important than the width, and connecting runs in a row can be cut down to ten feet or less in width if the length provided is ample.

The best surface for your run is a question open for argument. Breeders in Europe prefer packed-down fine cinders for their run surface, claiming

Modern living conditions make fencing and kenneling a necessity for the breeder. There are many makes of prefabricated runs, available from pet-shops and kennel supply houses that fill this need perfectly. Photo by Louise Van der Meid.

Sh. Ch. Ace of Acomb, owned by Mrs. D. A. W. Mucklow (England). Photo by C. M. Cooke and Son.

that this material provides good drainage and is the best surface for a dog's feet, keeping them compact and strong. Actually, heredity and, to a lesser degree, diet, are the prime factors that produce good feet in dogs, but a dog's feet will spread and lose compactness if he is kept constantly on a soft or muddy surface. Cinders do make an excellent run, but this surface also makes an admirable place in which the eggs and larvae of parasites can exist and thrive, and they are almost impossible to clean out from such a surface, short of resorting to a blowtorch. Here in America we favor cement runs. They are easy to clean and present a good appearance. But again, we have a porous surface into which the minute eggs of parasites can take refuge. Only by daily scrubbing with a strong disinfectant, or periodic surface burning, can concerte runs be kept free of these eggs and larvae.

Gravel and plain dirt runs present the same disadvantage, plus the difficulty of efficiently gathering stools from such surfaces. Dirt runs also become muddy in rainy weather and dusty in dry weather, making it necessary to change bedding often, and producing, as formerly mentioned, a deleterious effect upon the animal's feet. It would seem, then, that none of these run surfaces is the perfect answer to our problem. But there is yet another run surface which can give us better control over parasitic infestation. On this run we employ washed builders' sand for the surface. The dog generally defecates in a limited area, almost always at the end of this run farthest from the run door and his own house. Stools can easily be removed from the sand surface, and by digging down and removing one or two inches of sand below the stool, parasitic invaders are also removed. Fresh sand is filled into the spaces left by cleaning. The sand soon packs down and becomes a solid surface. The grains drop easily from the dog's feet and are not carried into his house to soil his bedding. This sand is not expensive, and periodically the whole surface can be removed and fresh sand brought in and leveled. An ideal run would be one with a cement base which can be washed down with disinfectants or a strong borax solution (which will destroy hookworm larvae) whenever the surface sand is completely removed and before a fresh sand surface is provided.

BUILDING YOUR RUN

If you plan to build the run yourself, you might consider the "soil-cement" surface as a base rather than true cement. Soil-cement is a subsurface employed on light-traffic airfields and many suburban roads; it is inexpensive, durable, and easily built without special knowledge or equipment. First remove the sod on the area to be converted into a run, then loosen the soil to a depth of about four inches with a spade and pulverize the soil, breaking up any lumps with a rake. Scatter dry cement at the rate of two-thirds of a sack of cement to a square yard of surface and mix in thoroughly with the soil until the mixture has a floury texture. Adjust your hose to a mist spray and water the surface until the soil-cement mixture will mold under pressure, and not crumble. Follow by raking the entire mixture to full depth to assure uniform moisture, and level at the same time. Now you must work quickly, compacting the run with a tamper and then rolling with a garden roller. All this must be done within a half hour or the surface will harden while still uneven. After rolling, the surface should be smooth and even. Mist-spray again, then cover with a coating of damp sawdust or soil for a week, after which the run can be used. Remember to keep a slight slope on all run surfaces so that water can drain off without puddling. Soil-cement is also excellent for paths around, or to and from, the kennels.

CLEANING YOUR RUN

In removing stools from a run, never rake them together first. This practice tends to spread worm eggs over a greater area. Shovel each stool up separately, and deposit it in a container. When the run is clean, carry the container to a previously prepared pit, dump the contents, and cover with a layer of dirt. Hose out the container and apply disinfectant, and the job is done with a minimum of bother. In winter, due to snow and ice, very little can be done about run sanitation. But those who live in climates which have definite and varied seasons have the consolation of knowing that worm eggs do not incubate nor fleas develop during cold weather. Therefore they must only do whatever is possible in run cleanliness for the sake of appearance and to keep down odors.

FENCING YOUR RUN

Fencing the run is our next problem. The ideal fencing is heavy chain link with metal supporting posts set in cement, and erected by experts. But

Cuede's Silver Dust, owned by Don Mitchell, and bred by Don Eddington.

Ch. Schmidt's Valiant Knight, owned by William E. Schmidt, and bred by Robert W. Mathews. Sire: Ch. Val Knight Ranck; dam: Ch. Gerda Aus der Grau. Photo by Joe Humphreys.

if your pocketbook cries at such an expenditure (and the cost is not small), you can do your own fencing, cutting the cost drastically by purchasing cheaper wire, using cedar posts for supports, and girding your loins for a bit of labor. Hog wire, six-inch stay wire fencing, fox wire, or fourteen gauge, or two-inch-mesh poultry wire all can be used. Whatever fencing you employ, be sure it is high enough to rise six feet above ground level and is of a heavy enough gauge to be substantial. A mature Weimaraner can easily scale fencing which is less than six feet high. Dig post holes, using horizontally stretched string as a guide to keep them evenly in line, and dig them deeply enough to hold the posts securely. Leave approximately six feet of space between each post hole. Paint the section of the post which is to be buried in the hole with creosote, or some other good wood preservative and set the posts in the holes. Concrete and rock, poured into the hole around the post,

Ch. Samantha of Saratoga Heights, U.D.T., owned by Leland and Marjorie Salisbury, and bred by Billy Curtis. Sire: Bitsu von Basha; dam: Silver Lady of Darlington. This bench and obedience winner is shown with her handler Harold Correll. Photo by Evelyn Shafer.

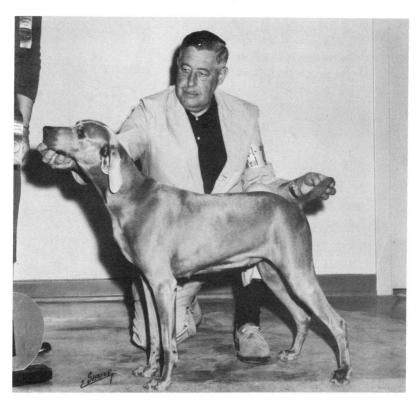

will provide a firm base. A horizontal top rail strengthens the run materially and will make for a better job. Brace all corner and gate posts. When your posts are in and set, borrow a wire stretcher for use in applying the wire fencing to the posts. This handy instrument can make the difference between a poor and a good job.

YOUR DOG HOUSE

The dog house can be simple or elaborate, reaching the extremes from a barrel set on cement blocks, to a miniature human dwelling, complete with shingles and windows. The best kind of house comes somewhere in between these two extremes. Build the house large enough, with sleeping quarters approximately three by five feet, and three feet high at the highest point. Incorporate a front porch one and a half to two feet deep and the five-foot width of the house. If the house is correctly situated, the porch roof offers shade from the sun and the porch itself a place to lie in rainy or snowy weather. Make the skeleton framework of two-by-threes, first building the two side

A new puppy should have a bed of its own, in the same way that an adult Weimaraner should have proper sleeping quarters. Photo by Louise Van der Meid.

Most people who use Weimaraners for hunting, find it better for their dogs to be housed in kennels than to be kept in the home. For the person who owns a number of dogs a kennel, with proper runs is a true necessity. Photo by Louise Van der Meid.

sections, allowing six inches of extra height on the uprights for floor elevation. Incorporate the porch size in the over-all length of the side pieces and remember the back slope over the sleeping portion, which will accommodate the hinged roof.

Next build the floor frame and cover it with five-eighths-inch outdoor plywood, or tongue and groove siding. Cover the sides with the same material you use for the floor. If you allow your two-by-three inch framing to show on the outside of the house, you will have a smooth inner surface to attach your floor platform to. Keep the floor the six inches above ground level provided by your side uprights and brace the floor by nailing six-inch pieces of two-by-threes under the floor and to the inside bottom of the side uprights. Frame in the door section between the porch and the sleeping quarters, framing for a door four to six inches from the floor (to hold in the bedding), eighteen inches wide and twenty-four inches high. Nail your plywood, or tongue and groove siding, over this framework, of course leaving the opening for the door, and nail the same wood across the back and the porch roof, thus closing the house in all around except for the roof section over the sleeping quarters. Build this section separately, with an overlay of four inches on the two sides and the back. Attach an underneath flange of wood on both sides and the rear, in from the edges, so that the flanges will fit snugly along the three outside edges of the house proper to keep out drafts and cold. Hinge this roof section to the back edge of the porch roof and cover the entire roof part with shingles or heavy tar paper, with a separate ten-inch flap stripped along and covering the hinged edge. Paint the house (blue or blue-gray paint is said to discourage flies), and it is finished.

If you wish, you may insulate with board insulation on the inside, or double flooring can be provided with insulating paper between the layers. In cold weather a gunny sack or a piece of canvas, rug or blanket, should be tacked at the top edge of the doorway to fall across the opening, thus blocking out cold air. If the house is big enough, an inside partial wall can be provided at one side of the door, essentially dividing the inner portion into a front hall with a weather-blocking partition between this hall and the sleeping quarters. If you build the house without the porch, you will find it necessary to build a separate platform on which the dog can lie outside in the sun after snow or rain. Should your ambitions embrace a full-sized kennel building with office, etc., it might be wise to investigate the prefabricated kennel buildings which are now on the market.

This house that you build, because of its size, is not an easy thing to handle or carry, so we suggest that you build it as close to the site you have picked for it as possible. The site should be at the narrow end of the run, with just a few inches of the porch jutting into the run and the greater bulk of the house outside of the run proper. Situate the house at the door end of the run, so that when you approach the run, the dog will not track through his excreta, which will be distributed at the end of the run farthest from the door. Try to set the house with its side to the north and back to the west. This gives protection from the coldest compass point in winter and shades the porch in summer from the hot afternoon sun.

A house built to the dimensions advised will accommodate two fully grown Weimaraners comfortably if the weather-block partition is eliminated, or one mature dog if it is not. Remember that the smaller and lower you can build your house without cramping your dog, the warmer it will be in the winter. If the house is not too large, is well built, and the doorway blocked adequately, you will be surprised by the amount of heat the dog's body will generate in cold weather to keep his sleeping quarters warm. To house several dogs, the necessary number of houses can be built or, if you so wish, one house doubled in length, with a dividing partition and two doorways, to service two separate runs.

Bedding for the sleeping box can consist of marsh grass, oat, rye, or wheat straw, or wood, pine, or cedar shavings. The last is said to discourage fleas and lice and possesses an aromatic odor. Shake a liberal supply of flea powder in the bedding once a week or each time the bedding is changed. The bedding may be changed once a month, but should be changed more often in rainy or muddy weather. Old bedding should be burned so it will not become a breeding place for parasites. Periodically the dog house should be cleaned out, washed with soap and water and a good disinfectant, and aired with the hinged roof section propped open.

GROOMING

Grooming should be a pleasant experience and a time of silent and delightful communication between you and your dog. Try to find the time to groom your Weimaraner once every day. It should take only a few minutes of your time, except during the season of shedding. By removing dead hair, dust, and skin scales in the daily grooming, you keep your Weimaraner's coat glossy, his appearance neat. This kind of daily grooming also eliminates the necessity of frequent bathings. For ordinary grooming use a wire grooming glove and finish with a stiff-bristled brush (not nylon). During the shedding season, a coarse-toothed hacksaw blade pulled through the coat is handy for removing loose hair below the coat surface, while an ordinary rubber heel, applied with the curved inside edge against the coat, will help remove loose hair on the surface. During the grooming procedure, beginning skin disease can be seen and nipped in the bud. The best grooming tools are those designed specifically for the job at hand; these are available at your pet shop.

The Weimaraner's short, smooth coat is a simple matter to groom. A brief daily session with a brush is usually sufficient to keep the Weimaraner's coat in good order. Photo by Louise Van der Meid.

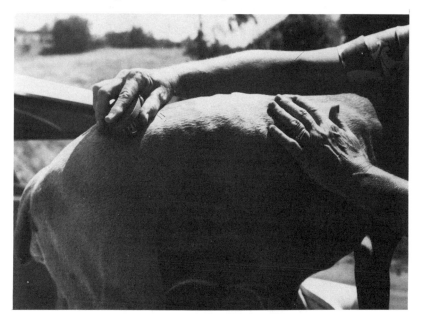

BATHING

You may bathe your dog or puppy any time you think it necessary, as long as you do not think it is necessary too frequently. Be careful in chilly weather to bathe him in a warm room and make sure he is completely dry before you allow him to venture out into the cold outdoors. When you bathe your dog, you soak him down to the skin and remove the protective oils from his coat. When a dog is exposed to rain and snow, the dampness is shed by the outer coat. Therefore he is not likely to be affected by natural seasonal conditions. Be careful, however, that he is not exposed to these same conditions directly after a bath, as there is danger of his contracting a cold. During the time of shedding, a bath once a week is not too often if the weather is warm. It helps to remove loose hair and skin scales, as does the grooming that should follow the bath when the dog is completely dry. As mentioned above, your Weimaraner's coat is water-resistant, so the easiest way to insure the removal of deep dirt and odors caused by accumulated sebum is by employing a chemicalized liquid soap with a coconut-oil base. Some commercial dog soaps con-

It is wise to put a drop of mineral oil in each eye of the dog before bathing it. In this way the risk of shampoo stinging the eyes is reduced, this is doubly important with young puppies. Photo by Louise Van der Meid.

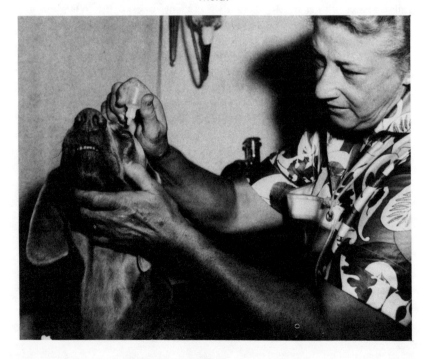

A plug of cotton in each ear will keep water out of them during the bath and will avoid possible ear trouble later. Photo by Louise Van der Meid.

tain vermin poisons, but an occasional prepared pesticidal dip, after bathing and rinsing, is more effective and very much worth while. When bathing, rub the lather in strongly down to the skin, being careful not to get soap in the dog's eyes. Cover every inch of him with heavy lather, rub it in, scrape the excess off with your hands, rinse and dry thoroughly, then walk him in the sun until he is ready for grooming. There are paste soaps available that require no rinsing, making the bathing of your Weimaraner that much easier, or you may wish to use liquid detergents manufactured specifically for canine bathing. Prepared canned lathers, as well as dry shampoos, are all available at pet shops and are all useful in keeping your Weimaraner clean and odorless.

There are many dog people who do not believe in frequent bathing because it tends to remove the oil from the dog's coat and can result in dry skin, dandruff, and skin itch. If you are in this category and wish to keep your Weimaraner clean and fresh-looking without fully bathing him, you can do so by employing the following procedure. First, fill a pail with lukewarm water and swish a bar of a bland cosmetic soap through the water until it is very slightly cloudy. Dip a large towel in the water and throw it over your Weimaraner's back in much the same manner as a drying blanket is draped over a horse. Begin rubbing the moisture through your Weimaraner's coat from behind his ears down his neck, back, croup, etc., until you have rubbed him all over and completely. Then rinse the towel in fresh water, wring it out, and repeat the procedure until the first liquid application has been completely removed. Following this, rub the dog down briskly with a dry towel, comb him, combing in the direction of the lay of his coat, and allow him to dry in the sun if possible. Do not permit him to roll in dirt or earth, a habit which seems to be the particular delight of most dogs after bathing or grooming.

If your dog has walked in tar which you find you cannot remove by bathing, you can remove it with kerosene. The kerosene should be quickly removed with strong soap and water if it is not to burn and irritate the skin. Paint can be washed off with turpentine, which must also be quickly removed for the same reasons. Some synthetic paints, varnishes, enamels, and other like preparations, which are thinned with alcohol, can be removed by the same vehicle. If the paint (oil base) is close to the skin, linseed oil will dissolve it without irritation. Should your Weimaraner engage in a tête-a-tête with a skunk, wash him immediately (if you can get near him) with soap and hot

The body of the dog should be wet down first. A dog will tend to be quieter if the body is wet before the head. Photo by Louise Van der Meid.

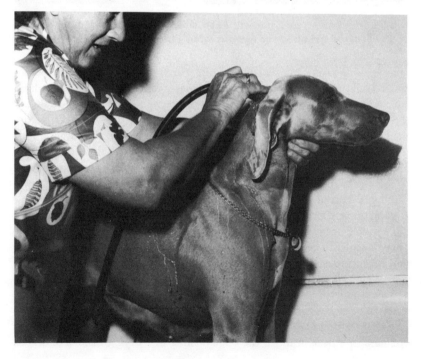

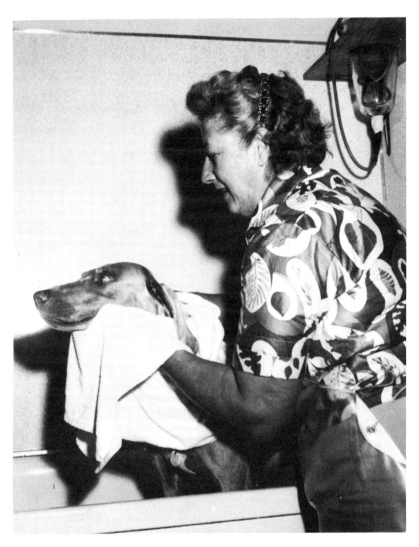

After the bath, all excess mosture should be removed before the dog is lifted from the tub. This makes drying much faster and easier, not to mention avoiding a wet floor. Photo by Louise Van der Meid.

water, or soak him with tomato juice if you can find enough available, then walk him in the hot sun. The odor evaporates most quickly under heat.

A box of small sticks with cotton-tipped ends, which are manufactured under various brand names, are excellent for cleaning your dog's ears. Drop into the ear some propylene glycol, or a mixture of ether and alcohol, to dissolve dirt and wax, then swab the ear clean with the cotton-tipped stick. Surplus liquid will quickly evaporate.

CARE OF CLAWS AND TEETH

Keep your dog's claws trimmed short. Overgrown claws cause lameness, foot ailments, spread toes, and hare feet. If your dog does a great deal of walking on cement, claw growth is often kept under control naturally by wearing off on the cement surface. Some Weimaraners seem to possess a genetic factor for short claws which never need trimming, but the majority of our dogs need claw care. To accomplish this task with the least possible trouble, use a cutter specifically designed to trim canine claws and cut away only the horny dead section of the claws. If you cut too deeply, you will cause bleeding. A flashlight held under the claw will enable you to see the

The claws of the dog should be shortened with clippers especially designed for the purpose. Care should be taken not to sever the vein that runs through the center of each claw, as profuse bleeding will result. Photo by Louise Van der Meid.

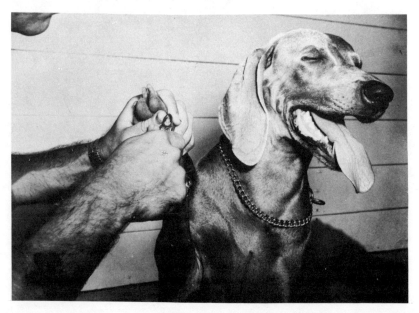

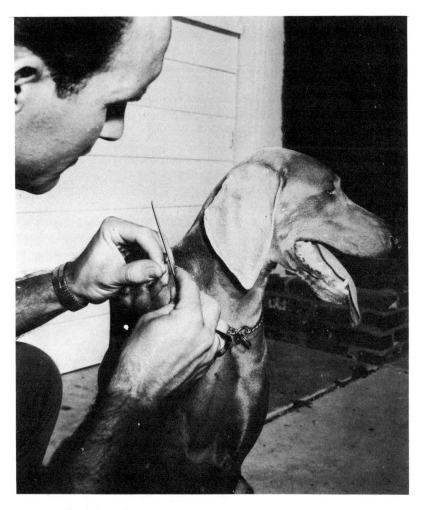

After the claws have been shortened they may be filed with an instrument especially designed for dogs. If the vein, or quick, has been cut, however, the claw should not be filed for at least twenty-four hours. Photo by Louise Van der Meid.

dark area of the blood line so you can avoid cutting into it. If you should tap the blood supply in the claw, don't be overly alarmed, simply keep the dog quiet until the severed capillaries close and the bleeding stops. Munsel's solution or a styptic pencil applied to the bleeding claw helps to hurry coagulation. After you have cut the claws, file them smooth with the use of a specially designed file. File from above with a downward, rounding stroke. If a claw has bled from trimming, do not file it for at least twenty-four hours. (Technically speaking a dog has claws, not nails, a fact attested to by the common term "dewclaws." Nails, as typified by the human fingernail, are

In the event that the vein in a dog's claw has been severed, a coagulant should be applied until the bleeding stops. Photo by Louise Van der Meid.

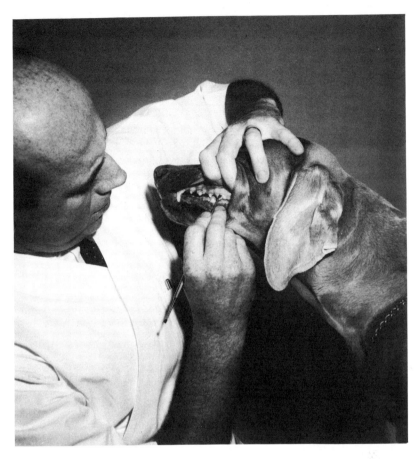

A dog's teeth should receive regular attention. Any accumulation of tartar should be removed with a dental tooth scraper. Photo by Louise Van der Meid.

flat and of a different construction microscopically.)

Soft rib bones fed twice a week will help prevent tartar from forming on your dog's teeth. His teeth pierce the bones, scraping off tooth residue in the process, keeping his teeth clean and white. If tartar should form, it can be chipped off with the same kind of instrument your dentist uses on your teeth for that purpose, or your veterinarian can clean them efficiently and without bother to you. Check your dog's mouth every other week for broken, loose, or abscessed teeth, particularly when he has passed his prime. Bad teeth must be tended by your veterinarian before they affect your dog's general health. Rawhide and nylon bones, available at pet shops, remove tartar also, and are even safer.

FLIES

During the summer months certain flies, commonly called "deer" flies, bite at the tips of a dog's ears, causing great discomfort, the formation of scabs, subsequent baldness, and sometimes infection in that area. A good liquid insecticide, one of the many recently developed for fly control, should be rubbed or sprayed on the dog's ears, as often as necessary to keep these pests away. Skin-disease salve which contains sulphur and oil of turpentine as a vehicle is also efficacious against flies, particularly if D.D.T. flea powder is shaken on top of the salve, where it adheres, giving extra protection. Oil of benzoin and oil of cade, painted on the ears, are also effective.

RATS

If rats invade the kennel area, they should be eradicated as quickly as

An ounce of prevention **IS** worth a pound of cure. Periodic checks for the presence of external parasites should be a regular part of every dog's routine. Petshops now carry many good insecticides, packaged in aerosol spray cans, making application a simple matter for the control of fleas, lice, ticks, and other insect pests. Photo by Louise Van der Meid.

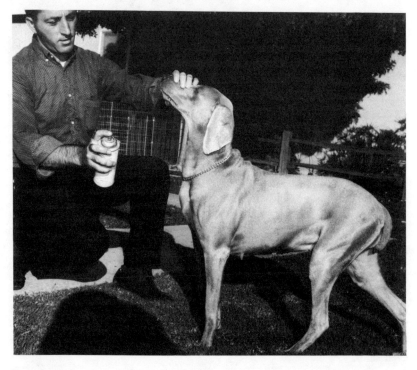

Many Weimaraner owners have found that wire crates make very pactical traveling arrangements for their dogs. In this way, the dog does not annoy human passengers, and is protected from any injury in the event of an unexpected short stop. Photo by Louise Van der Meid.

possible. Not only are they disease carriers, but they are an affront to our more delicate senses. To get rid of them, set out small pans of dog meal near their holes every night for several nights until you have them coming to these pans to feed. Then mix red squill with the dog food they are being fed, eight measures of dog meal to one of red squill. After a single night's feeding of this poisonous mixture, you will generally rid your premises of these gray marauders. Red squill is a drug that is relatively nonpoisonous to all animals except rodents, so it can be used around the kennel with safety.

TRAVEL

When traveling in hot weather with your dog, never leave him in a closed car in the sun alone. Death takes its grisly toll each summer of dogs so treated. Carry his water pail and food dish with you and take care of his needs as you do your own when on the road. If you intend changing his diet to one more easily fed when traveling, begin the change a few days before your trip so he can become accustomed to it. Gaines Research Division publishes a list of approximately 3,500 hostelries across the country that will accept dogs: a handy booklet for the dog-loving traveler to have.

If you find it necessary to ship a Weimaraner to another section of the country, make sure the crate you use is large enough in all dimensions to keep the dog from being cramped during his journey. Check to see that there are no large openings or weak sections which might break in transit and allow the dog's limbs to project out of the crate. Consult your veterinarian or your local express agency for data on state health certificates. Supply the dog with a pan, rigidly attached to the crate, for water, and throw a few dog biscuits on the floor of the crate for the dog to gnaw during his journey to alleviate boredom. Be sure there are air holes in strategic locations to provide air and ventilation. If possible, the top surface of the crate should be rounded, rather than flat, to discourage the parking of other crates on top of the dog crate. Strips of wood, nailed horizontally along the outside of the crate and projecting out from the surface, will prevent adjacent crates, or boxes, from being jammed tightly against the dog crate and thus blocking and defeating the purpose of the ventilation holes.

A periodic health check of your Weimaraner by your veterinarian can pay big mental and monetary dividends. When you take him for his examination, remember to bring with you samples of his stool and urine for analysis.

EXERCISE

Exercise is one of the facets of canine care that is many times neglected by the owner. The Weimaraner, in particular, needs his share of muscular activity if he is to develop properly that floating, easy gait which is a part of his breed being. Dogs need a great deal more exercise than humans, so taking your dog for a walk on leash cannot be considered exercise from the canine standpoint. If you can allow him to run free when you take him out, he will get more exercise, but still just a bare modicum of what is necessary. If you teach him to chase a ball and retrieve it, he will get still more exercise, while you can take your ease. But the best way to provide a Weimaraner with correct and substantial exercise is to train him to trot beside a bicycle. In this manner he will receive the steady movement which will give him co-ordination, muscular fluidity, and tightness. Begin this type of exercise at about seven months. At this age, a mile a day is sufficient. Train him to run at the right side of the bicycle, to protect him from traffic. As he grows older, the amount of ground covered should increase, so that at maturity he is covering five to six miles a day with comparative ease. Pedal slowly, keeping the dog in an easy, relaxed, and even trot, and when he shows signs of weariness, stop and lie on roadside grass to rest until it is time to resume again. If the weather is exceptionally hot, it is best to skip the exercise for that day, or wait until

Swimming is an excellent form of exercise for a Weimaraner. Being a natural water dog, he takes to it more readily than many breeds. The Weimaraner that lives near water is indeed lucky. Photo by Annette Samuels.

the cool of evening. Many owners who live in rural areas and allow their dogs the freedom of several acres can assume that the animal is getting enough exercise by himself. The Weimaraner that is hunted also gets his full measure of exercise. The above relates to the pet or show dog.

We have considered in this chapter the elements of physical care, but we must not forget that your Weimaraner needs mental care as well. His character and mental health need nourishment, grooming, and exercise, just as much as his physical being. Give him your companionship and understanding, teach him right from wrong, and treat him as you would a friend whom you enjoy associating with. This, too, is a part of his general care, and perhaps the most important part for both you and your Weimaraner.

Remember that good general care is the first and most important part of canine ownership and disease prevention. The health and happiness of your Weimaraner is in your hands. A small amount of labor each day by those hands is your dog's health and life insurance, and the premium is paid by your Weimaraner in love and devotion.

Chapter VII
The Brood Bitch

If we want to succeed in improvement within our breed, we must have an even greater trueness to breed type in our bitches than we have in their breeding partners. The productive value of the bitch is comparatively limited in scope by seasonal vagary and this, in turn, increases the importance of every litter she produces.

To begin breeding we must, of necessity, begin with a bitch as the foundation. The foundation of all things must be strong and free from faults, or the structure we build upon it will crumble. The bitch we choose for our foundation bitch must, then, be a good bitch, as fine as we can possibly acquire, not in structure alone, but in mentality and character as well. She is a product of her germ plasm, and this most important facet of her being must be closely analyzed so that we can compensate, in breeding, for her hidden faults. Structurally, the good brood bitch should be strongly made and up to standard size. She should be deep and not too long in body, for overlong bitches are generally too long in loin and weak in back, and after a litter tend to sag in back line. She must possess good bone strength throughout, yet she should not be so coarse as to lack femininity. Weakness and delicacy are not the essence of femininity in our breed and should be particularly avoided in the brood bitch.

Your bitch will first come in season when she is between eight and twelve months of age. Though this is an indication that nature considers her old enough and developed enough to breed, it is best to allow her to pass this first heat and plan to breed her when she next comes in season. This should come within six months if her environment remains the same. Daylight, which is thought to affect certain glands, seems to influence the ratio of time between heats, as will complete change in environment. Scientific studies of the incidence of seasonal variation in the mating cycles of bitches indicate that more bitches come in heat and are bred during the months of February through May than at any other time of year. The figures might not be completely reliable, since they were assembled through birth registrations in the A.K.C., and many breeders refrain from fall and winter breedings so they will not have winter or early spring litters. Small breeds reach maturity much earlier than do our Weimaraners.

A bitch of good bloodlines is the breeder's most important tool for the production of outstanding animals. In the Weimaraner, the breeder aims for a dog of high intelligence, great physical beauty, and an inborn bird sense. The Weimaraner is a dual purpose dog, and can excell on the bench, in the field, or in obedience equally well. This dual dog is the breeder's goal.

Ch. Leer's Jan Tomerlin and her litter, owned by W. S. and A. M. Tomerlin. The sire of these sturdy youngsters is Ch. Jomar's Rock and Roll.

In Germany, a bitch is not bred until she has passed two seasons, but it is not necessary to wait this long. In fact, should you breed your bitch at her second season, it will probably be better for her, settling her in temperament and giving her body greater maturity and grace.

When your bitch is approaching her period of heat and you intend to breed her, have her stool checked for intestinal parasites, and if any are present, worm her. Feed her a well-balanced diet, such as she should have been getting all along. Her appetite will increase in the preparatory stage of the mating cycle as her vulva begins to swell. She will become restless, will urinate more frequently, and will allow dogs to approach her, but will not allow copulation. Within the bitch other changes are taking place at this stage.

Congestion begins in the reproductive tract, and the horns of the uterus and the vagina thicken.

The first sign of blood from the vulva ushers in the second stage of the mating cycle. In some bitches no blood appears at all, or so little that it goes unnoticed by the owner, and sometimes we find a bitch who will bleed throughout the cycle. In either circumstances we must depend upon other signs. The bitch becomes very playful with animals of her own, and the opposite sex, but will still not permit copulation. This is, of course, a condition which is very trying to male dogs with which she comes in contact. Congestion within the bitch reaches a high point during this period. Ova develop within the follicles of the ovaries, and, normally, the red discharge gradually turns to pink, becoming lighter in color until it becomes straw color and is no longer obvious. Her vulva is more swollen, and she becomes increasingly more playful with males. This period is generally of about ten days' duration, but the time varies greatly with the individual. Rather than rely upon any set time period, it is best to conclude that this period reaches its conclusion

Crook 'N' Nanny's Silver Faun, C.D., S.D.X., owned and bred by Jean Budler. Sire: Sir Butte of Wimar; dam: Duchess Florian Grey. Faun is shown going best of winners at Chicago International.

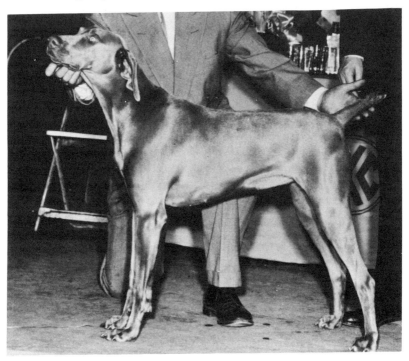

when the bitch will stand for the stud and permit copulation. This generally occurs at about the tenth day, but can take place as early as the fourth or fifth day of this period or as late as the seventeenth day.

The third period in the cycle is the acceptance period. The bitch will swing her hind end toward the dog, her tail will arch and fall to the side, and she will permit copulation. Sometimes the stud may have to tease her for a time, but she will eventually give in. The bitch may be sensitive and yelp and pull away when the stud's penis touches the lining of the vagina. If this occurs several times, it is best to wait another day, until the sensitivity has left this region. A very definite indication that the bitch is in the acceptance period is the softness and flaccidity of the vulva, from which the firmness and congestion has gone. Within the bitch the ovarian follicles have been growing ever bigger, and approximately midway in the acceptance period, some of them burst and the eggs are ready for fertilization. If the bitch has a normal mating cycle, which is to be hoped for, the best time to breed her is about the thirteenth or fourteenth day of the mating cycle, when ovulation has occurred. This time also varies with the individual bitch, so that until you have bred your bitch once or twice and feel that you know the best time for her, it is better to breed her on the eleventh day and every other day thereafter until her period of acceptance is over. This last, of course, is generally only possible when the stud is owned by you. One good breeding is actually all that is necessary to make your bitch pregnant, providing that breeding is made at the right time. If copulation is forced before the bitch is ready, the result is no conception or a small litter, since the sperm must wait for ovulation and the life of the sperm is limited. The acceptance period ceases rather abruptly, and is signaled by the bitch's definite resistance to male advances.

If your bitch is a maiden, it is best to breed her this first time to an older stud who knows his business. When you bring her to the stud and if there are adjoining wire-enclosed runs, put the stud in one run and the bitch in the adjacent one. They will make overtures through the wire and later, when the stud is loosed in the run with the bitch, copulation generally occurs quickly. You may have to hold the bitch if she is flighty or reluctant, sometimes a problem with maiden bitches. If your bitch fails to conceive from a good and proper breeding, do not immediately put the blame on the stud. In most instances it is the fault of the bitch or, more realistically, the owner of the bitch for not adequately timing the mating. Many bitch owners fail to recognize the first signs of the mating cycle and so bring their bitch to the stud either too early or too late. Normal physiology of the reproductive system can be interrupted or delayed by disturbance, disease, or illness in any part of the dog's body. A sick bitch will therefore generally not come in season, though it is time to do so, until after she has completely recovered and returned to normal. Bitches past their prime and older tend to have a shorter mating

Ch. Helmanhof's Storm Cloud, owned by Mrs. Helms Crutchfield, is shown winning best of breed at the Virginia Kennel Club. He is shown with his handler, Johnny Davis.

Ch. Gwinner's Telestarwheel, owned and bred by Tony P. and Beatrice S. Gwinner. Sire: Ch. Ann's Ricky Boy, C.D.; dam: Ch. Cati v.d. Gretchenof. Telestarwheel is shown finishing to his championship at the Glendale Kennel Club under judge George Higgs, Mr. Gwinner handling. Photo by Wentzle Ruml.

cycle and so must be bred sooner than usual to assure pregnancy.

During copulation and the resulting tie, you should assist the stud dog owner as much as possible. If the stud evidences pain when he attempts to force his penis into the vulva, check the bitch. In virgin bitches you may find a web of flesh which runs vertically across the vaginal opening and causes pain to the dog when his penis is forced against it. This web must be broken by hooking your finger around it and pulling if a breeding is to be consummated. After the tense excitement of the breeding and while the tie is in effect, speak to the bitch quietly and keep her from moving until the tie is broken, then snap a leash onto her collar and take her for a fast walk around the block without pausing. After that she can be taken home in the car. If it is necessary to travel any great distance before she arrives again in familiar surroundings, it is best to allow her a period of quiet rest before attempting the journey.

Occasionally fertile bitches, whether bred or not, will have phantom pregnancies and show every physical manifestion of true gestation up to the last moment. In some cases a bitch may be truely bred and then, after a month, resorb her fetuses. The only way of differentiating between pseudo-pregnancy and fetal resorbtion is by palpation, or feeling with the hands, to locate the fetal lump in the uterus. This is a difficult task for one who has not had vast experience.

After you have returned home with your bitch, do not allow any males near her. She can become impregnated by a second dog and whelp a litter of mixed paternity, some of the puppies sired by the first dog and others sired by the second animal. Often a bitch is bred to a selected stud just before ovulation. The sperm will live long enough to fertilize the eggs when they flush down. The next day, another male breeds to the bitch, the sperm of the two dogs mix within her and both become sires of the resulting litter.

Let us assume that your bitch is in good health and you have had a good breeding to the stud of your choice at the proper time in the bitch's mating cycle to insure pregnancy. The male sperm fertilizes the eggs and life begins. From this moment on you will begin to feed the puppies which will be born in about sixty to sixty-three days from ovulation. Every bit of food you give the bitch is nutritionally aiding in the fetal development within her. Be sure that she is being provided with enough milk to supply calcium, meat for phosphorus and iron, and all the other essential vitamins and minerals. A vitamin and mineral supplement should be incorporated into the food, but used moderately. Alfalfa leaf meal of twenty-four per cent protein content may become part of the diet. She must be fed well for her own maintenance and for the development of the young *in utero*, particularly during the last thirty days of the gestation period. She should not, however, be given food to such excess that she becomes fat.

Your bitch, her run, and house or bed should be free of worm and flea eggs. She should be allowed a moderate amount of free exercise in the prenatal period to keep her from becoming fat and soft and from losing muscular tone and elasticity. If your bitch has not had enough exercise prior to breeding and you wish to harden and reduce her, accustom her to the exercise gradually, and it will do her a great deal of good. But do not allow her to indulge in unaccustomed, abrupt, or violent exercise, or she might abort.

The puppies develop in the horns of the uterus, not in the "tubes" (Fallopian tubes), as is commonly thought. As the puppies develop, the horns of the uterus lengthen and the walls expand until the uterus may become as long as three and a half feet in a Weimaraner bitch carrying a large litter. A month before the bitch is due to whelp, incorporate fresh liver in her diet two or three times a week. This helps to keep her free from constipation and aids in the coming, necessary production of milk for the litter. If the litter is going to be small, she will not show much sign until late in the gestation period. But if the litter is going to be a normal or large one, she will begin to show distention of the abdomen at about thirty-five days after the breeding. Her appetite will have been increasing during this time, and gradually the fact of her pregnancy will become more and more evident.

Several days before she is due to whelp, the whelping box should be prepared. It should be located in a dimly lit area removed from disturbance by other dogs, or humans. The box should be four feet square, enclosed on all sides by eight- to ten-inch high boards, either plank or plywood. Boards of the same height must be added above these in about three weeks to keep the pups from climbing out. Four inches up from the flooring (when it is packed down), a one- by three-inch smooth wooden slat should be attached to the sides with small angle irons, all around as a rail, or a pipe rail can be used. This will prevent the bitch from accidentally squeezing to death any puppy which crawls behind her. On the floor of the box lay a smooth piece of rubber matting which is easily removed and cleaned when the bedding is cleaned or changed. The bedding itself should be of rye or oat straw, and enough of it supplied so that the bitch can hollow out a nest and still leave some of the nesting material under the pups. Another method much used is to have several layers of newspapers in the bottom of the box so that they can be removed one or two at a time as they become soiled during whelping. After the litter is completely whelped, the straw bedding is provided and hollowed into a saucer shape so the whelps will be kept together in a limited area. The whelping box should be raised from the ground and a smaller box, or step provided, to make it easier for the bitch to enter or leave.

As the time approaches for the whelping, the bitch will become restless; she may refuse food and begin to make her nest. Her temperature will drop approximately one degree the day before she is ready to whelp, and she will

A proper whelping box will incorporate, among other things a "pig rail." This simple wood rail all around the inside of the whelping box will prevent the dam from accidentally leaning on a puppy and smothering it to death. Photo by Annette Samuels.

show a definite dropping down through the abdomen. Labor begins with pressure from within that forces the puppies toward the pelvis. The bitch generally twists around as the puppy is being expelled to lick the fluid which accompanies the birth. Sometimes the sac surrounding the puppy will burst from pressure. If it doesn't, the puppy will be born in the sac, a thin, membranous material called the fetal envelope. The navel cord runs from the puppy's navel to the afterbirth, or placenta. If the bitch is left alone at whelping time, she will rip the fetal caul, bite off the navel cord and eat the sac, cord, and placenta. Should the cord be broken off in birth so that the placenta remains in the bitch, it will generally be expelled with the birth of the next whelp. After disposing of these items, the bitch will lick and clean the new puppy until the next one is about to be born, and the process will then repeat itself. Under completely normal circumstances, your Weimaraner bitch is quite able to whelp her litter and look after them without any help from you, but since the whelping might not be normal, it is best for the breeder to be present, particularly so in the case of bitches who are having their first litter.

If the breeder is present, he or she can remove the sac, cut the umbilical cord, and gently pull on the rest of the cord, assuming that the placenta has

Ch. Skyfield's Beau of Talbot, owned by Lillian and Edward Larsen and bred by Joachim E. Welcher. Sire: Fritz von Bruderliebstadt; dam: Skyfield's Misty Morning.

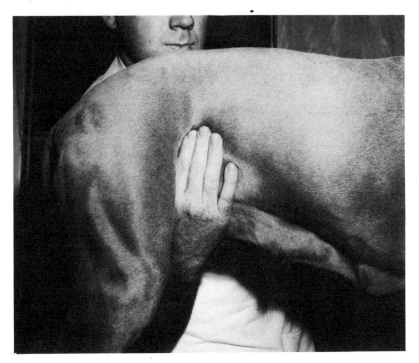

When a bitch is about four or five weeks in whelp, the unborn puppies may be felt by careful palpitation. This should only be attempted by a veterinarian or experienced breeder. Poking around by a novice can result in grave trouble. Photo by Louise Van der Meid.

not yet been ejected, until it is detached and drawn out. Some breeders keep a small box handy in which they place each placenta, so they can, when the whelping is completed, check them against the number of puppies to make sure that no placenta has been retained. The navel cord should be cut about three inches from the puppy's belly. The surplus will dry up and drop off in a few days. There is no need to tie it after cutting. You need not attempt to sterilize your hands or the implements you might use in helping the bitch to whelp, since the puppies will be practically surrounded with bacteria of all kinds, some benign and others which they are born equipped to combat.

If a bitch seems to be having difficulty in expelling a particularly large puppy, you can help by wrapping a towel around your hands to give you purchase, grasping the partly expelled whelp, and gently pulling. Pull very, very gently, or you might injure the puppy. The puppies can be born either head first or tail first. Either way is common. As the pups are born, the sac broken, and the cord snipped, dry them gently but vigorously with a towel and put them at the mother's breast, first squeezing some milk to the surface and then opening their mouths for the entrance of the teat. You may have to hold them there by the head until they begin sucking.

Often several puppies are born in rapid succession, then an interval of time may elapse before another one is born. If the bitch is a slow whelper and seems to be laboring hard after one or more pups have been born, regular injections of Pitocin, at three-hour intervals, using a little less than one-half c.c., can help her in delivery. Pituitrin, one-half to one c.c., is a similar drug and the one most often used, though Pitocin brings less nausea. Both these drugs should be administered hypodermically into the hind leg of the bitch at the rear of the thigh. After the bitch has seemingly completed her whelping, it is good practice to administer another shot of the drug to make sure no last puppy, alive or dead, is still unborn and to cause her to clean out any residue left from the whelping. Never use either of these drugs until she has whelped at least one puppy.

Allow her to rest quietly and enjoy the new sensation of motherhood for several hours, then insist that she leave her litter, though she won't want to, and take her out to relieve herself. Offer her some warm milk. From then on, feed her as recommended during the gestation period, with the addition of three milk feedings per day. Sometimes milk appears in the udders before birth, but generally it comes in when the pups begin to nurse, since it is manufactured by glands, from blood, while the puppies are at the breast.

Now is the time to cull the litter. Of course, all young which are not normal should be culled immediately at birth. If the bitch whelps six or less puppies and all seem strong and healthy, no culling is required. If she has a particularly large litter, it does not pay, in the long run, to raise all the whelps. Allow her to keep six or seven of the best and sturdiest and cull the rest. Those which you have retained will grow better and be larger and stronger than if you allowed the entire large litter to live. Quiet puppies are healthy ones. Constant crying and squirming of the pups is a danger signal, and a check should be made to see what ails them. It may be that the bitch is not providing enough milk and they are hungry, or perhaps they are cold. Sometimes the trouble is parasitic infection, or possibly coccidiosis, or navel infection. Dr. Walter Koch, in 1950, at the University of Munich, Animal Institute, reported a bacillus, *Aerogenes*, which he claimed caused many deaths of young puppies. This bacillus infects from contact with the dam's rectum. It multiplies rapidly in the whelp's intestines, and the normal bacilli in the stomach and intestines seem to have no effect on the lethal bacillus. It begins with the first digestion of the puppies and attacks the basic internal organs, exhibiting symptoms on the second or third day following birth. The puppies develop cramps, fail to suck, whimper, and die within two or three days. The disease does not seem to be contagious to other well puppies. If there is something wrong with the puppies, whatever it may be,

A six-week old Weimaraner puppy on point. A puppy like this is truly a joy to the breeder. A youngster that shows such early promise of skill in the field will probably be an ideal shooting dog all its life.

Wave of Mortgaged Acres and one of her puppies. Wave is owned by Mrs. Helms Crutchfield and was bred by Jack Baird. Photo by Annette Samuels.

you need professional advice and should call your veterinarian immediately.

Except for the removal of dewclaws and tail docking, the puppies, if healthy, need not be bothered until it is time to begin their supplementary feeding at about three weeks. Dewclaws should be removed and tails docked on about the second day after birth. Puppies and their needs, dietary and otherwise, are discussed more fully in a later chapter.

There are several ills which might befall the bitch during gestation and whelping which must be considered. Eclampsia, sometimes called milk fever, is perhaps most common. This is a metabolic disturbance brought on by a deficiency of calcium in the diet. If you give your bitch plenty of milk and a good diet such as we have recommended, she should not be troubled with this condition. Should your bitch develop elcampsia—evidenced by troubled shaking, wild expression, muscular rigidity, and a high temperature —it can be quickly relieved by an injection of calcium gluconate in a vein.

Should your bitch be bred by accident to an undesirable animal, your veterinarian can cause her to abort by the use of any one of several efficient canine abortifacients. He can also aid old bitches who have been resorbing their fetuses to carry them full term and whelp with the aid of stilbestrol.

Mastitis, an udder infection, is a chief cause of puppy deaths. It is generally mistaken by the uninformed for "acid milk," a condition which does not exist in dogs because the bitch's milk is naturally acid. Mastitis is an udder infection which cuts off part of the milk supply and the whelps either die of infection, contracted from the infected milk, or from starvation, due to the lack of sufficient milk. It is not necessary to massage the dam's breasts at weaning time with camphorated oil. They will cake naturally and quickly quit secreting milk if left completely alone.

Growths, infections, injuries, cysts, and other and various ailments can effect the female reproductive system and must be taken care of by your veterinarian. The great majority of bitches who have been well cared for and well fed are strong and healthy, and the bearing of litters is a natural procedure: the normal function of the female of the species to bear and rear the next generation, and in so doing fulfill her precious destiny.

Chapter VIII
The Stud Dog

A famous German breeder wrote: "Modern breeding research has taught us that it is not so much the appearance of an animal that indicates its breeding values, but rather its hereditary picture, which means the sum total of the qualities and characteristics which it has inherited from its ancestors." This statement is as true today as when it was written in 1930, and is particularly applicable to the stud dog.

If what we have said above about the unrivaled importance of the brood bitch is true, it may be difficult to understand why we pay so much attention to the male lines of descent. The reason is that stud dogs tend to mold the aspects of the breed on the whole and in any given country, or locality, to a much greater extent than do brood bitches. While the brood bitch may control type in a kennel, the stud dog can control type over a much larger area. The truth of this can be ascertained by the application of simple mathematics.

Let us assume that the average litter is comprised of five puppies. The brood bitch will produce, then, a maximum of ten puppies a year. In that same year a popular, good producing, well-publicized stud dog may be used on the average of three times weekly (many name studs, in various breeds, have been used even more frequently over a period of several years). This popular stud can sire fifteen puppies a week, employing the figures mentioned above, or 780 puppies a year. Compare this total to the bitch's yearly total of ten puppies, and you can readily see why any one stud dog wields a much greater influence over the breed in general than does a specific brood bitch.

The care of the stud dog follows the same procedure as outlined in the chapter on general care. He needs a balanced diet, clean quarters, and plenty of exercise, but no special care as does the brood bitch. Though it is against most of the advice previously written on the subject, we recommend that the stud be used in breeding for the first time when he is about twelve months old. He is as capable of siring a litter of fine and healthy pups at this age as he ever will be. He should be bred to a steady, knowing bitch who has been bred before, and when she is entirely ready to accept him. Aid him if necessary this time first. See that nothing disturbs him during copulation. In fact,

Ch. Gronbach's Aladdin, C.D., owned by Robert Gronbach, is a sire of fine champions, as well as a top winner in his own right. Photo by Deford Dechert.

the object of this initial breeding is to see that all goes smoothly and easily. If you succeed in this aim, the young dog will be a willing and eager stud for the rest of his life, the kind of stud that it is a pleasure to own and use.

After this first breeding, use him sparingly until he has reached sixteen or seventeen months of age. After that, if he is in good health, there is no reason why he cannot be used at least once a week or more during his best and most fertile years.

The male organs vital for reproduction consist of a pair each of: testicles, where the sperm is produced; epididymis, in which the sperm are stored; and vasa deferentia, through which the sperm are transported. The dog possesses no seminal vesicle as does man. But, like man, the male dog is always in an active stage of reproduction and can be used at any time.

When the stud has played with the bitch for a short period and the bitch is ready, he will cover her. There is a bone in his penis, and behind this bone is a group of very sensitive nerves which cause a violent thrust reflex when pressure is applied. His penis, unlike most other animals', has a bulbous enlargement at its base. When the penis is thrust into the bitch's vagina, it goes through a muscular ring at the opening of the vagina. As it

The ideal stud dog should be typically masculine, of good disposition, yet bold, and of course, pleasing to the eye. All things are not as important though as the stud's bloodline, which can only be judged by past progeny. Photo by Louise Van der Meid.

The owners of many studs often use their dogs' winning as a selling point for his desirability as a producer of winners. Many top dogs are top sires, but this is not always true. Photo by Louise Van der Meid.

passes into the vagina, pressure on the reflex nerves causes a violent thrust forward, and the penis, and particularly the bulb, swells enormously, preventing withdrawal through the constriction band of the vulva. The stud ejaculates semen swarming with sperm, which is forced through the cervix and uterus, into the Fallopian tubes, and the breeding is consummated.

The dog and bitch are tied, or "hung," and the active part of the breeding is completed. The owner of the bitch should then stand at her head and hold her by the collar. The stud's owner should kneel next to the animals with his arm or knee under the bitch's stomach, directly in front of her hindquarters, to prevent her from suddenly sitting while still tied. He should talk soothingly to the stud and gently prevent him from attempting to leave the bitch for a little while. Presently the stud owner should turn the dog around off the bitch's back by first lifting the front legs off and to the ground and then lifting one hind leg over the back of the bitch until dog and bitch are standing tail to tail.

Dogs remain in this position for various lengths of time after copulation, but fifteen minutes to a half an hour is generally average. When the congestion of blood leaves the penis, the bulb shrinks and the animals part.

The stud dog owner should keep a muzzle handy to be used on snappy bitches. Many bitches, due to temperament, environment, or fright, may cause injury to the stud by biting. If she shows any indication of such conduct, she should be muzzled. Should she continue to attempt to bite for any length of time, it is generally because it is either too early or too late in the estrum cycle to consummate a breeding. If the bitch is small, sinks down when mounted, or won't stand, she must be held up. In some instances her owner or the stud's owner will have to kneel next to her and, with his hand under and between her hind legs, push the vulva up toward the dog's penis or guide the stud's penis into her vulva. Straw or earth, pushed under her hind legs to elevate her rear quarters, is effective in the case of a bitch who is too small for the stud.

As mentioned before, many novice bitch owners fail to recognize the initial signs of the oncoming heat period, or neglect to check, so that their knowledge of elapsed time since the first showing of red is only approximate. Many offer little aid in the attempt to complete the breeding, and talk incessantly and to no purpose, generally expressing wonder at their bitch's unorthodox conduct, but do little to quiet her. In many instances, particularly with a novice of the opposite sex, these actions are due to embarrassment. Regardless of the reason, remember to use the muzzle only on the bitch. We must always put the welfare of our dogs ahead of self.

There is not much more that can be written about the stud, except to caution the stud owner to be careful of using drugs or injections to make his dog eager to mate or more fertile. The number of puppies born in any litter is not dependent upon the healthy and fertile male's sperm, but upon the number of eggs the bitch gives off. Should your dog prove sterile, look for basic causes first. If there seems to be no physical reason for his sterility, then a series of injections by your veterinarian (perhaps of A-P-L, anterior-pituitary-like, hormone) might prove efficacious.

It is often a good idea to feed the dog a light meal before he is used, particularly if he is a reluctant stud. Young, or virgin, studs often regurgitate due to excitement, but it does them no harm. After the tie has broken allow both dog and bitch to drink moderately.

Perhaps it would be well, in this chapter dealing with the stud, to discuss something which is closely related to the sexes and breeding: breed surveys.

Breed surveys have marked value if properly and objectively conducted. The basic idea of the breed survey (or *Angekoert*) is to evaluate your dog impartially so that you, the owner, can see him in true perspective, minus the blind spots which come to most breeders and owners and are the result of close familiarity. The first phase of the breed survey is a professional criticism of both physical and mental faults and virtues. The second phase is a recommendation concerning breeding partners, warning the breeder to

Dual Ch. Greta von Kallerplatz, S.D.X., owned by Ted and Lori Jarmie, and bred by Herbert D. Hoon. Greta is the only Weimaraner bitch in the history of the breed to hold a bench and a field championship.

guard against breeding to strains or individuals carrying certain genetic weaknesses which are also prevalent in the animal being surveyed. The eternal argument against breed surveys is that they represent only the opinions of a limited group of individuals who may or may not be completely qualified to give opinions. In Germany, breed surveys have immense value and the evaluations and recommendations are seldom criticized. But breed surveys have much less impact in America because of our way of living, thinking, and acting.

We have had breed surveys before in this country, but their value was made nil by a general disregard of recommendations, and the movement died of inertia. Should a group of truly knowledgeable breeders of undeniable integrity and intelligence be gathered together for a breed survey, and the individuals making the survey be changed yearly, we would, in all probability, eventually have a worth-while picture of existing stock. It is quite possible that such a group could be formed and, over the years, make a necessary contribution to breed knowledge. But regardless of how accurately it might recommend and classify, it would be bucking American individuality, ego, and stubbornness against being pushed into a direction decided by others. We respect the findings and opinions of our peers, but insist upon our own decisions. Like the proverbial horse, we can be led to water, but we cannot be forced to drink. Undeniably, this attitude must be exasperating to any group or groups who are, without profit or glory, attempting to set our steps on the right path. But it must be also remembered that many a horse has been founded by drinking too quickly and too much.

Chapter IX
Your Weimaraner Puppy

The birth of a litter has been covered in a previous chapter on the brood bitch. As we indicated in that discussion, barring accident or complications at birth, there is little you can do for your Weimaraner puppies until they are approximately three weeks old. At that age supplementary feedings begin. But suppose that for one reason or another the mother must be taken from her brood. What care must be given to these small Weimaraners if they are to survive? Puppies need warmth. This is provided partly by their instinctive habit of gathering together in the nest, but to a much greater extent by the warmth of the mother's body. If the mother must be taken from the nest, this extra warmth can be provided by an ordinary light bulb, or, better still, an infra-red bulb, hung directly over the brood in the enclosed nest box.

By far the most important requirement of these newborn puppies is proper food. Puppies are belly and instinct, and nothing much more. They must be fed well and frequently. What shall we feed them, what formula can we arrive at that most closely approaches the natural milk of the mother, which we know is best? There are prepared modified milks for orphan puppies which are commercially available and very worth while, or you can mix your own formula of ingredients which will most closely simulate natural bitch's milk. To do this, you must first know the basic quality of the dam's milk. Bitches' milk is comparatively acid; it contains less sugar and water, more ash and protein, and far more fat than cow or human milk, so we must adjust our formula to conform to these differences.

To begin, purchase a can of Nestle's Pelargon, a spray-dried, acidified, and homogenized modified milk product. If you can't get Pelargon, try any of the spray-dried baby milks, but Pelargon is best since it is, like bitches' milk, slightly acid and rich in necessary nutritive substances. To one ounce of the modified milk product, add one ounce of fresh cream. Pour six ounces of water by volume into this mixture and blend with an electric mixer or egg beater until it is smooth. Larger amounts can be mixed employing the same basic proportions and kept refrigerated. This formula should be fed five or six times a day and, when fed, must be warmed to body heat. Many puppies refuse to drink a formula that has not been warmed to just the

While he grows into a big, rugged field dog, the Weimaraner should receive careful, intelligent care as a puppy. If there are children in the household, they should learn how to properly look after the new pet. Photo by Louise Van der Meid.

Television, newspapers, and other media have helped to popularize purebred dogs. Cuede's Silver Dust, and his owner, Don Mitchell, do their part to bring the Weimaraner into greater prominence. "Corky the Clown" assists by holding a pair of young litter sisters.

right temperature. Do not add lime water, glucose, or dextrose to the formula, for by so doing you are modifying in the wrong direction. An ordinary baby's bottle and nipple are adequate as the formula vehicle. Never drop liquids directly in the puppy's throat with an eye dropper or you invite pneumonia. A twelve-ounce puppy will absorb one ounce of formula; a one-pound puppy, approximately one and three-quarter ounces of formula; a two-pound puppy, two ounces; and a three-pound puppy, two and three-quarter ounces at each feeding. A valuable adjunct to the puppy's diet, whether formula or breast fed, is two drops of Dietol, dropped into the lip pocket from the first day of birth on, the amount to be increased with greater growth and age. A bottle trough can be built for orphan puppies. The trick here is to space the nipple holes so that the bodies of the puppies touch when drinking.

If it is possible to find a foster mother for orphan puppies, your troubles are over. Most lactating bitches will readily take to puppies other than their own if the new babies are first prepared by spreading some of the foster mother's milk over their tiny bodies. The foster mother will lick them clean and welcome them to the nest.

When the pups are two and a half to three weeks old, the mother will often engage in an action which might prove slightly disgusting to the neophyte,

A sleek, healthy-looking puppy is its own best advertisement.

but which is an instinctive and natural performance to the bitch. She will regurgitate her own stomach contents of partially digested food for her puppies to eat, thus beginning, in her own way, the weaning process. If you have begun supplementary feeding in time, this action by the bitch will seldom occur. If you haven't, it is a definite indication that supplementary feeding should begin at once.

Puppies grow best on milk, meat, fat, and cereal diets. Growth is attained through proteins, but proteins differ, so that puppies fed on vegetable protein diets will not grow and thrive as well as those fed animal proteins. Vitamins E and K (found in alfalfa meal) are essential to the puppies' well being and should be used in adequate amounts in the food ration. Remember that seventy percent of the puppy's energy is derived from fat intake, so supply this food element generously in the diet. Lime water should not be incorporated into the diet since it neutralizes stomach acidity, a condition which is necessary to the assimilation of fat. In experiments, puppies on fat-free diets developed deficiency symptoms characterized by anemia, weight loss, dull coats, and finally, death. Fat alone could not cure the advanced manifestation of the condition, indicating that some metabolic process was disturbed when complete fat removal in the diet was resorted to. But feeding butterfat plus folacin resulted in dramatic cures.

To begin the small puppy on supplementary feeding, place the pan of food before him, gently grasp his head behind the ears, and dip his lips and chin into the food. The puppy will lick his lips, taste the food, and in no time at all learn to feed by himself. Be careful not to push the head in so far that the puppy's nose is covered and clogged by food.

Check the puppies' navels every day to see that infection has not set in. This infection comes from the scraping of their soft bellies on a rough surface and can generally be avoided if several thicknesses of cloth cover the floor of the nest box under the bedding.

Clip the sharp little claws to avoid damage to littermates' eyes, which will open at about ten days. If the puppies are born with hind dewclaws, cut them off with manicure scissors about two days after birth. They need not be bandaged, as the bitch will keep the wound clean until it has healed. Tails can be docked at this time too, or even earlier. Have a fecal check made when the puppies are about three-and-a-half weeks old. If they are infested with worms, worm them immediately. Do not attempt to build up the puppies first if the parasitic infestation has made them unthrifty. It is best to rid them of the worms quickly, after which they will speedily return to normal health and plumpness.

The weeks fly by, and before you know it the puppies are at salable age. The breeder, you can be sure, has not wasted these weeks. He has spent many hours in close observation of the litter and has centered his interest on one puppy which he thinks shows the most promise. Either he will hold this puppy for himself, sell him to a show-conscious buyer, or keep the puppy and sell it at a higher price when it has become more fully developed and its early promise becomes a fact. The strange part about this whole business of picking a young puppy from a litter is that the novice buyer many times stands as good a chance of picking the best puppy as the seasoned and experienced breeder. The reason for this seeming incongruity lies in the fact that in every litter there will be several puppies which, if well bred and well cared for, appear to be potential winners at eight to ten weeks of age. Another reason concerns the ratio of sectional growth in young animals. Each puppy, as an individual, will have a different growth rate and exhibit change in relative sections of the body, as well as in over-all growth, from day to day

If you are the potential purchaser of a Weimaraner puppy, or, for that matter, a grown dog, prepare yourself for the purchase first by attending as many shows and field trials as possible. Observe, absorb, and listen. Visit kennels that have well bred, winning stock, and at shows, trials, and kennels make an unholy nuisance of yourself by asking innumerable questions of people who have proved, by their record in the breed, that information gleaned from them can be respected. When you intend to purchase a new car, or an electrical appliance such as a refrigerator or washing machine, you go to sales rooms and examine the different makes, weighing their features and quality, one against the other. You inquire of friends who have different brands their opinion in regard to the utility value of the item, and, when you have made up your mind which brand is best, you make sure that you purchase the item from a reliable distributor. Do the same thing when you intend to purchase a dog. Before you make your journey to any breeder to buy a puppy, be sure to inquire first into the background of the breeder as well as the background of his dogs. What does this breeder actually know about his breed? What has he formerly produced? What is his reputation amongst other reputable breeders? Does his stock have balanced minds as well as balanced bodies? Find the answers to these questions even before you delve into the ancestry of the puppies he has for sale. If the answers prove that this breeder is an honest, dependable person with more than a smattering knowledge of the breed, and that he has bred consistently typical stock, then your next step will be to study the breeding of his puppies to determine whether they have been bred from worth-while stock which comes from good producing strains. Examine stock he has sold from different breedings to other customers. Be careful of kennels which are puppy factories, breeding solely for commercial reasons, and don't be carried away by hysterical, overdone, adjective-happy advertisements.

When you have satisfied yourself that the breeder is a morally responsible person who has good stock, then you may sally forth to a purchse your future

When the puppy is sold, the new owner should be given a pedigree, listing the dog's ancestors for at least three generations and the registration certificate, or application for registration. Photo by Louise Van der Meid.

champion. It is best, if possible, to invite an experienced breeder to accompany you on your mission. As mentioned before, even the most experienced breeder cannot with assurance pick the puppy in the litter which will mature into the best specimen. An experienced person can, however, keep you from selecting a very engaging youngster which exhibits obvious faults which quite possibly won't improve.

Assuming that the litter from which you are going to select your puppy is a fat and healthy one and it is a male puppy you have set your heart on having, ask the breeder to separate the sexes so you can examine the male puppies only. Normal puppies are friendly, lovable creatures wanting immediate attention, so the little fellow who backs away from you and runs away and hides should be eliminated from consideration immediately. This also applies to the puppy that sulks in a corner and wants no part of the proceedings. Watch the puppies from a distance of approximately twenty feet as they play and frolic, sometimes trotting and occasionally quitting their play for a fleeting moment to stand gazing at something of interest which has, for that second, engaged their attention. Don't be rushed. Take all the time necessary to pick the puppy you want. You are about to pay cold cash for a companion and a dependent who will be with you for many years.

If you have been lucky enough to have had the opportunity of examining both sire and dam, determine which puppies exhibit the faults of the parents or the strain. If any particular fault seems to be overdone in a specific pup, discard him from further consideration. Do not handle the puppies during this preliminary examination. Look for over-all balance first and the absence of glaring structural faults, but remember that the good pup will show an exaggeration of all the good points you expect to be present in the mature animal. Shy or frightened puppies (and grown dogs) have a tendency to crouch a bit. Watch the puppy's movement when at trot. A good one moves with a balanced, though ungainly, "bear cub" trot. Look particularly for a long reach in front, which indicates good shoulder angulation. Hindquarters often improve, except when the hock is straight and angulation is sorely lacking at this age, but front assemblies seldom change. A dog with good shoulders and reach can be depended upon to get the most from what he has when moving. Angulation, fore and aft, should be determined without handling, since a puppy has a tendency to crouch when set up for examina-

Crook 'N' Nanny's Rose Marie, owned by Marilyn Brodhagen, and bred by Marie Seidelman. Sire: Ch. Gourmet's Theron; dam: Ch. Crook 'N' Nanny's Silver Diana. Photo by Ritter.

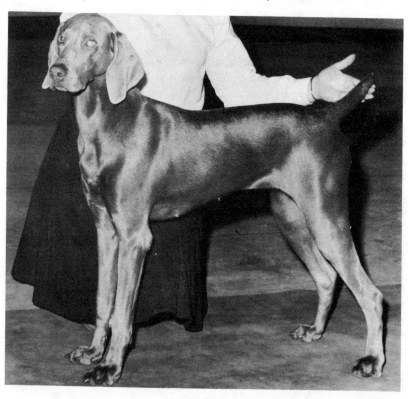

For trips to the veterinarian, puppy matches and any car excursion, it is advised that puppies be transported in wire crates. This procedure makes things easier on puppies, as well as passengers. Photo by Louise Van der Meid.

tion, exaggerating the angle of skeletal structure in these sections. The importance of the shoulder should be remembered by the novice, since the eye is usually first engaged by exaggerated rear angulation.

Make sure the back is short and straight, not roached or swayed. The ribs should be deep, well-sprung, and reaching far back, leaving a short, strong loin. The pup should be broad across the back and over the loin and croup, and the croup itself long and gently sloping to the tail. Many young puppies appear cow-hocked when standing if they possess very good or extreme rear-quarter angulation. This condition generally disappears with age, unless cowhocks is an inherited condition. Your Weimaraner puppy should exhibit a short hock, firm, well rounded and thickly padded feet, and heavy, strong bone. Avoid the puppy who appears too tight and finished or mature at this age; be careful, too, of the novice's delight, the biggest, loosest, and clumsiest pup in the litter. The former will lack size, bone, and masculinity at maturity, and the latter will quite often never attain compactness or true fluidity in movement.

By this time you have probably narrowed the field down to one or two puppies. It is time now to hand-examine the one or two youngsters who look the best to you. Stand each one upon a table individually in a show stance and examine the head, the ears, and the shape of skull and muzzle. Check whether the neck is dry and of correct length, and whether it sets properly into the shoulders. Then examine the mouth for tooth and jaw structure to determine the bite. An overshot pup frequently levels off with growth if it is not an hereditary anomaly and is slight; but an undershot jaw seldom corrects itself to any great extent by maturity. Next, attempt to determine if the puppy is sexually whole. At this age the testicles are descended into the scrotum, but are often drawn up when the puppy is being handled, making it difficult to locate both testicles during examination. The buyer should have a written agreement with the seller to the effect that, should the pup prove to be a monorchid or cryptorchid, the puppy can be returned and the purchase price refunded or the pup replaced by another of equal value.

If it is a female pup you want, look for the same values as outlined above in choosing a male. You would not, of course, go through the performance of determining sex as mentioned above. Female puppies are generally slightly smaller and show a degree of greater refinement than the males.

Remember that no one can pick a champion at eight weeks and no breeder can truthfully sell you a future winner at that age. All a breeder can guarantee is the health and breeding of the puppy, and the fact that he possesses the normal complement of eyes, ears and legs. The best you can do if you are observant, knowing, and lucky, is to pick the best puppy in that particular litter, at that particular time.

If it is at all possible, it is best to purchase two puppies at the same time. They furnish company for each other, eliminate lonesome serenades during the first few nights, and are competition at the food pan. If you bring home only one puppy, provide him with a stuffed dog or doll in his sleeping box which you have taken to the breeder's with you and rubbed in the nest box. This will frequently give the puppy some sense of comfort and companionship and alleviate lonesomeness that brings on dismal howling during the first night in his new home. A ticking alarm clock near the puppy's bed will sometimes have the same effect.

In his new home, amidst strange surroundings, the puppy will very often go off his feed for a time. This should not unduly alarm you unless his refusal to eat lasts so long that he becomes emaciated. If this occurs, ask your veterinarian for a good tonic, or change diets to tempt his palate. Never coax him or resort to forced feeding, or you will immediately spoil your puppy and be a slave to him and his aggravating eating habits from that time forward. If he eats only one or two meals a day, instead of the several feedings he should have, he will survive until his appetite improves if he is otherwise healthy and

Ch. Helmanhof's Sky Rocket, owned and bred by Mrs. Helms Crutchfield. This best in show dog was one of the top winners of the past. Photo by William Brown.

vigorous. Should you find after a reasonable time and much scheming and effort that you have a naturally finicky eater, you must resign yourself to the fact that you have acquired a headache which can last for the duration of your dog's life and one which cannot be cured by aspirin. Only heroic measures can help you conquer this difficulty, and you must steel yourself and cast out pity if you are to succeed. He must be starved, but really starved, until he has reached a point where dry bread resembles the most succulent beef. Only by such drastic measures can a finicky eater be cured. Dogs who have the competition of other dogs, or even a cat, at the feed pan usually display a normal appetite. For this reason it is sometimes smart for the one-dog owner to borrow a friend's or neighbor's pet to feed with his own until such time as his own dog has acquired a healthful and adequate appetite.

Arrange for your puppy to have lots of sleep, particularly after feeding, a difficult chore when there are youngsters in the home, but nevertheless very necessary to the well being of the pup. Make him feel at home so he will respond quickly to his new surroundings. It so often happens that a puppy retained by the breeder surpasses at maturity the purchased pup who was a better specimen in the beginning. This confounds the novice, yet has a reasonably simple explanation. The retained puppy had no change in environment which would affect his appetite and well being during the critical period of growth, while the bought puppy had and so was outstripped by his lesser litter brother.

Your puppy will have two sets of teeth, the milk teeth, which will have fallen out by the time he is approximately six months of age, and the permanent teeth, which he'll retain for the rest of his life. Loss of weight and fever may accompany the eruption of the new, permanent teeth, but is no cause for alarm. Zoologists have a simple formula to represent the number and arrangement of permanent teeth which, at a glance, will allow you to determine if your dog has his full complement of teeth, and if he hasn't, which ones are missing. In the chart below, the horizontal line represents the division between upper and lower jaw. We begin with the incisors in the front of the dog's mouth and designate them with the letter I. The canine teeth are labeled C, the premolars, P, and the molars, M. Formulas, for simplicity, generally only list the teeth from one side (right or left) of the head. As the teeth on the other side are a duplicate, by merely doubling the number in the formula you can obtain either the total number of each kind of tooth or the total number of teeth.

$$I_3^3 \ C_1^1 \ P_4^4 \ M_3^2 = \frac{10 \ (\times \ 2) = 20 \ \text{upper teeth}}{11 \ (\times \ 2) = 22 \ \text{lower teeth}} = 42 \ \text{teeth}$$

Occasionally, puppies develop lip warts which will disappear in a short time, leaving no aftereffects. Remember to have your puppy immunized against distemper and hepatitis and, as much as possible, keep him away from other dogs until he is old enough to combat the diseases which take their toll of the very young. Lastly, but of great importance, give your puppy the opportunity to develop that character and intelligence for which the Weimaraner is justly famed. Give him human companionship and understanding, take him with you in the car and amongst strangers. Let him live the normal happy, and useful life which is his heritage, and that tiny bundle of fur which you brought home so short a time ago will grow into a canine citizen of whom you will be proud to say, "He's mine."

Chapter X
Fundamental Training

Responsibility for the reputation of any breed is shared by everyone who owns a specimen of that breed. Reputation, good or bad, is achieved by conduct, and conduct is the result of the molding, through training, of inherent character into specific channels of behavior.

It is a distinct pleasure, to novice, old-timer, or the public at large, to watch dogs perform which have been trained to special tasks. Here is the ultimate, the end result of the relationship between man and dog. After watching an inspired demonstration, we sometimes wonder if, under a proper training regime, our own Weimaraner could do as well. Perhaps he can, if he is temperamentally fitted for the task we have in mind. No single individual of any breed, regardless of breed type, temperament, and inheritance, is fitted to cope with all the branches of specialized service. Nor does every

The Weimaraner's high order of intelligence is proven by the many fine obedience winners in the breed, often the same dogs that win on the bench, and in the hunting field. Photo by Annette Samuels.

173

owner possess the qualifications or experience necessary to train dogs successfully to arduous tasks. But every dog can be trained in the fundamentals of decent behavior, and every dog owner can give his dog this basic training. It is, indeed, the duty of every dog owner to teach his dog obedience to command as well as the necessary fundamentals of training which insure good conduct and gentlemanly deportment. A dog that is uncontrolled can become a nuisance and even a menace. This dog brings grief to his owner and bad reputation to himself and the breed he represents.

We cannot attempt, in this limited space, to write a complete and comprehensive treatise on all the aspects of dog training. There are several worth-

Rudi von Liechtenstein, C.D., owned by Lewis D. and Dorothea E. Chancey. and bred by Chrystal H. Spellerberg. Sire: Samson's Grey Ghost; dam: Heidi von Bachausen.

Good training should begin at as early an age as possible. One of the first and most important lessons is teaching the puppy to walk properly on leash. Photo by Louise Van der Meid.

while books, written by experienced trainers, that cover the entire varied field of initial and advanced training. There are, furthermore, hundreds of training classes throughout the country where both the dog and its owner receive standard obedience training for a nominal fee, under the guidance of experienced trainers. Here in these pages you will find only specific suggestions on some points of simple basic training which we feel are neglected in most of the books on this subject. We will also attempt to give you basic reasons for training techniques and explain natural limitations to aid you in eliminating future, perhaps drastic, mistakes.

The key to all canine training, simple or advanced, is control and understanding. Once you have established control over your Weimaraner, you can, if you so desire, progress to advanced or specialized training in any field. The dog's only boundaries to learning are his own basic limitations. This vital control must be established during the basic training in good manners.

Almost every Weimaraner is responsive to training. He loves his master and finds delight in pleasing him. To approach the training problem with your Weimaraner, to make it a pleasant and easy intimacy rather than an arduous and wearisome task, you must first learn a few fundamentals. In the preceding paragraph we spoke of control as an essential in training. To gain control over your dog, you must first establish control over your own vagaries of temperament. During training, when you lose your temper, you lose control. Shouting, nagging repetition, angry reprimand, and exasperation only confuse your canine pupil. If he does not obey, then the lesson has not been learned. He needs teaching, not punishment. The time of training should be approached with pleasure by both master and dog, so that both you and your pupil look forward to these periods of contact. If you establish this atmosphere, your dog will enjoy working, and a dog who enjoys his work, who is constantly trying to please, is a dog who is always under control.

Duskin's Princess Shellie, C.D.X., owned by Mr. and Mrs. Louis Pardo. This dog was shown to her obedience title by her owner and is also shown in the breed ring by her owner. Photo by Alexander.

The command "down" is quite useful in the control of a dog. This hand signal is often used in teaching this. Photo by Louise Van der Meid.

Consistency is the brother of control in training. Perform each movement used in schooling in the same manner every time. Use the same words of command or communication without variance. Employ command words that are simple single syllables, chosen for their crispness and difference in sound. Don't call your dog to you one day with the command "come," and the next day, with the command "here," and expect the animal to understand and perform the act with alacrity. Inconsistency confuses your dog. If you are inconsistent, the dog will not perform correctly and your control is lost. By consistency you establish habit patterns which eventually become an inherent part of your Weimaraner's behavior. Remember that a few simple commands, well learned, are much better than many and varied commands only partially absorbed. Therefore be certain that your dog completely understands a command and will perform the action it demands, quickly and without hesitation, before attempting to teach him a new command.

Before we begin training, we must first assess our prospective pupil's intelligence and character. We must understand that his eyesight is not as keen as ours, but that he is quick to notice movement. We must know that sound and scent are his chief means of communication with his world, and that in these departments he is far superior to us. We must reach him, then, through voice and gesture, and realize that he is very sensitive to quality change and intonation of the commanding voice. Therefore, any given command must have a definite tonal value in keeping with its purpose. The word "no" used in reprimand must be expressed sharply and with overtones of displeasure, while "good boy," employed as praise, should be spoken lightly and pleasantly. In early training, the puppy recognizes distinctive sound coupled with the quality of tone used rather than individual words.

All words of positive command should be spoken sharply and distinctly during training. By this we do not mean that commands must be shouted, a practice which seems to be gaining favor in obedience work and which is very much to be deplored. A well-trained, mature Weimaraner can be kept completely under control and will obey quickly and willingly when commands are given in an ordinary conversational tone. The first word a puppy learns is the word-sound of his name; therefore, in training, his name should be spoken first to attract his attention to the command which follows. Thus, when we want our dog to come to us, and his name is Kurt, we command, "Kurt! Come!"

The scent discrimination exercise is designed to test a dog's perception and keenness of smell. It is used in utility classes and is a popular feature of all obedience trials. Photo by Louise Van der Meid.

Intelligence varies in dogs as it does in all animals, human or otherwise. The ability to learn and to perform is limited by intelligence and facets of character and structure, such as willingness, energy, sensitivity, aggressiveness, stability, and functional ability. The sensitive dog must be handled with greater care and quietness in training than the less sensitive animal. Aggressive dogs must be trained with firmness; an animal which possesses a structural fault which makes certain of the physical aspects of training a painful experience cannot be expected to perform these acts with enjoyment and consistency.

Training begins the instant the puppies in the nest feel the touch of your hand and are able to hear the sound of your voice. Once the puppy is old enough to run and play, handle him frequently, petting him, making a fuss over him, speaking in soothing and pleasant tones and repeating his name over and over again. See chapter 13 for use of whistle and gun during puppyhood for field training. When you bring him his meals, call him by name and coax him to "come." As time passes, he associates the command "come" with a pleasurable experience and will come immediately upon command. Every time he obeys a command, he should be praised or rewarded. When calling your puppies to their food, it is good practice to use some kind of distinguishing sound accompanying the command—a clucking or "beep" sound. It is amazing how this distinctive sound will be retained by the dog's memory, so that years after it has ceased to be used, he will still remember and respond to the sound.

Some professional trainers and handlers put soft collars on tiny puppies, with a few inches of thin rope attached to the collar clip. The puppies, in play, tug upon these dangling pieces of rope hanging from the collars of their littermates, thus preparing the youngsters for easy leash breaking in the future. In training the puppy to the leash, be sure to use a long leash, and coax, do not drag, the reluctant puppy, keeping him always on your left side. Never use the leash as an implement of punishment.

Housebreaking is usually the tragedy of the novice dog owner. We who have Weimaraners are fortunate in this respect since, as a breed, they are basically clean in habit and quite easily housebroken. Many Weimaraners that are raised outside in a run never need to be actually housebroken, preferring to use the ground for their act and seemingly sensing the fact that the house is not to be soiled. Dogs tend to defecate in areas which they, or other dogs, have previously soiled, and will go to these spots if given the chance. Directly after eating or waking a puppy almost inevitably has to relieve himself. If he is in the house and makes a mistake, it is generally your fault, as you should have recognized these facts and removed him in time to avert disaster. If, after you have taken him out, he comes in and soils the floor or rug, he must be made to realize that he has done wrong. Scold him with, "Shame! Shame!" and rush him outside. Praise him extravagantly when he has taken advantage of the great outdoors. Sometimes if you catch him preparing to void in the house, a quick, sharp "no" will stop the proceedings and allow you time to usher him out. Never rub his nose in his excreta. Never indulge in the common practice of striking the puppy with a rolled up newspaper or with your hand. If you do, you may be training your dog either to be hand shy, to be shy of paper, or to bite the newsboy. Your hand should be used only in such a way that your dog recognizes it as that part of you which implements your voice, to pet and give pleasure. In housebreaking, a "no" or "shame" appropriately used and delivered in an admonishing tone is punishment enough.

Dogs which attain the size of a Weimaraner are seldom broken to paper in the house. If your dog has been so trained and subsequently you wish to train him to use the outdoors, a simple way to teach him this is to move the

If your Weimaraner is paper broken, he can be switched to the outdoors by putting his papers out, and in this way giving him the idea that "this must be the place." Photo by Louise Van der Meid.

In teaching a dog to take the broad jump, the handler should take the jump with the dog, and the dog should be leashed until he gets the idea. Photo by Louise Van der Meid.

paper he has used outside, anchoring it with stones. Lead the dog to the paper when you know he is ready to void. Each day make the paper smaller until it has completely disappeared, and the puppy will have formed the habit of going on the spot previously occupied by the paper. Puppies tend to prefer to void on a surface similar in texture to that which they used in their first few weeks of life. Thus a puppy who has had access to an outside run is easily housebroken, preferring the feel of ground under him. Smaller breeds are sometimes raised on wire-bottom pens to keep them free of intestinal parasites. Occasionally puppies so raised have been brought into homes with central heating employing an open grate-covered duct in the floor. To the puppy the grate feels similar to his former wire-bottomed pen. The result, as you can well imagine, gives rise to much profanity and such diligence that the youngster is either rapidly housebroken or just as rapidly banished to live outdoors.

If your Weimaraner is to be a housedog, a lot of grief can be avoided by remembering a few simple rules. Until he is thoroughly clean in the house, confine him to one room at night, preferably a tile- or linoleum-floored room that can be cleaned easily. Tie him so that he cannot get beyond the radius of his bed, or confine him to a dog house within the room; few dogs will soil their beds or sleeping quarters. Feed at regular hours and you will soon learn the interval between the meal and its natural result and take the puppy out in time. Give water only after meals until he is housebroken. Puppies, like inveterate drunks, will drink constantly if the means is available, and there is no other place for surplus water to go but out. The result is odd puddles at odd times.

"No," "shame," "come," and "good boy" (or "girl"), spoken in appropriate tones, are the basic communications you will use in initial training.

If your pup is running free and he doesn't heed your command to come, do not chase him, he will only run away or dodge your attempts to catch him and your control over him will be completely lost. Attract his attention by calling his name and, when he looks in your direction, turn and run away from him, calling him as you do so. In most instances he will quickly run after you. Even if it takes a great deal of time and much exasperation to get him to come to you, never scold him once he has. Praise him instead. *A puppy should be scolded only when he is caught in the act of doing something*

The "sit" is one of the most important exercises a dog can learn. To teach it, the trainer should have the dog at his left side, pressing on the dog's loin with one hand, and pulling on the lead with the other, all the time commanding "sit." Photo by Louise Van der Meid.

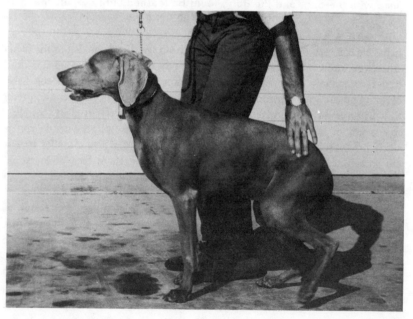

No dog should be allowed to sit on furniture meant for people. When the habit is broken in puppyhood, it is not likely to appear in the adult. Photo by Louise Van der Meid.

he shouldn't do. If he is scolded even a few minutes after he has committed his error, he will not associate the punishment with the crime and will be bewildered and unhappy about the whole thing, losing his trust in you.

Puppies are inveterate thieves. It is natural for them to steal food from the table. The "no" and "shame" commands, or reprimands, should be used to correct this breach of manners. The same commands are employed when the puppy uses your living room couch as a sleeping place. Many times dogs are aware that they must not sleep on the furniture, but are clever enough to avoid punishment by using the sofa only when you are out. They will hastily leave the soft comfort of the couch when they hear you approaching and greet you in wide-eyed innocence, models of canine virtue. Only the tell-tale hair, the dent in the cushion, and the body heat on the fabric are clues to the culprit's dishonesty. This recalls the tale of the dog who went just a step further. So clever was he that when his master approached, he would leap from the couch and, standing before it, blow upon the cushions to dislodge the loose hair and cool the cushion's surface. The hero of this tale of canine duplicity was not identified as to breed, but we are sure that such intelligence could only have been displayed by a Weimaraner.

If, like the dog in the story, the puppy persists in committing this misdemeanor, we must resort to another method to cure him. Where before we used a positive approach, we must now employ a negative, and rather sneaky, method. The idea is to trick the puppy into thinking that when he commits these crimes he punishes himself and that we have been attempting to stop him from bringing this punishment down upon his head. The use of mousetraps is a neat little trick to cure the persistent sofahopper. Place two or three set traps on the couch area the dog prefers and cover with a few sheets of newspaper. When he jumps up on the sofa, he will spring the traps and leave that vicinity in a great and startled hurry.

With the unregenerate food thief, tie a tempting morsel of food to a long piece of string. To the string attach several empty tin cans, or small bells, eight to ten inches apart. Set the whole contraption on the kitchen or dining-room table, with the food morsel perched temptingly on an accessible edge. Leave the room and allow the little thief to commit his act of dishonesty. When you hear the resultant racket, rush into the room, sternly mouthing the appropriate words of reproach. You will generally find a thoroughly chastened puppy who, after one or two such lessons, will eye any tabled food askance and leave it strictly alone.

These methods, or slight variations, can be used in teaching your puppy to resist many youthful temptations such as dragging and biting rugs, furniture, tablecloths, draperies, curtains, etc.

The same approach, in essence, is useful in teaching the puppy not to jump up on you or your friends and neighbors. You can lose innumerable friends if your mud-footed dog playfully jumps up on the visitor wearing a new suit or dress. If the "no" command alone does not break him of this habit, hold his front legs and feet tightly in your hands when he jumps up, and retain your hold. The puppy finds himself in an uncomfortable and unnatural position standing on his hind legs alone. He will soon tug and pull to release his front legs from your hold. Retain your hold in the face of his struggles until he is heartily sick of the strained position he is in. A few such lessons and he will refrain from committing an act which brings such discomfort in its wake.

Remember that only by positive training methods can you gain control which is the basis of successful training, and these tricky methods do not give you that control. They are simply short-cut ways of quickly rectifying nuisance habits, but do nothing to establish the rapport which must exist between trainer and dog.

Teach your Weimaraner always to be friendly with other people. The protective instinct is strongly inherited in our breed and specific training to develop it is not generally needed.

During the entire puppy period the basis is being laid for other and more

184

advanced training. The acts of discipline, of everyday handling, grooming, and feeding, are preparation for the time when he is old enough to be taught the meaning of the "sit," "down," "heel," "stand," and "stay" commands, which are the first steps in obedience training and commands which every dog should be taught to obey immediately. Once you have learned how to train your dog and have established complete control, further training is only limited by your own abilities and by the natural boundaries that exist within the animal himself.

Don't rush your training. Be patient with small progress. Training for both you and your dog will become easier as you progress. Make sure that whatever you teach him is well and thoroughly learned, and it will never be forgotten. Remember that your dog's inherited character and intelligence form certain limiting patterns.

Let us review the few and basic truths set forth in this chapter. Remember to use simple common sense when you approach the task of training. Approach it with ease and confidence. Control yourself if you wish to control your dog, for control is the vital element in all training. Realize the limitations as well as the abilities of your dog, and the final product of your training zeal will bring you pride in accomplishment, pride in yourself and your ability, and pride in your Weimaraner.

As in the broad jump, the high jump is taught by the handler taking the jump with the dog the first few times, using the command "over." The dog is eventually expected to take the jump alone, and off leash. Photo by Louise Van der Meid.

Ch. Jan's Countess Rowena, owned by W. S. and Agnes Tomerlin and bred by W. S. Tomerlin. Sire: Ch. Jomar's Rock and Roll; dam: Ch. Leer's Jan Tomerlin, S.D.X., R.D.X. This trim bitch is seen winning best of opposite sex from the classes at the Weimaraner Club of America, held with Harbor Cities, under judge Virgil Johnson, handler Jack Dexter. Photo by Joan Ludwig.

Chapter XI
Training for the Show Ring

So many things of beauty or near perfection are so often marred and flawed by an improper approach to their finish. A Renoir or an El Greco tacked frameless to a bathroom wall is no less a thing of art, yet loses importance by its limited environment and presentation. Living things, too, need this finish and preparation to exhibit their worth to full advantage. The beauty of a flower goes unrecognized if withered petals and leaves mar its perfection, and the living wonder of a fine dog is realized only in those moments when he stands or moves in quiet and balanced beauty. The show ring is a ready frame in which to display your dog. The manner in which he is presented within that frame is up to you.

If you contemplate showing your Weimaraner, as so many of you who read this book do, it is of the utmost importance that your dog be as well and fully trained for exhibition as he is for general gentlemanly conduct in the home. Insufficient or improper training, or faulty handling, can result in lower show placings than your dog deserves and can quite conceivably ruin an otherwise promising show career. In the wider sense, and of even more importance to the breed as a whole, is the impression your Weimaraner in the show ring projects to the gallery. Every Weimaraner shown becomes a representative of the breed in the eyes of the onlookers, so that each dog becomes a symbol of all Weimaraners when he is on exhibition. Inside the ring ropes, your dog will be evaluated by the judges as an individual; beyond the ropes, a breed will be judged by the behavior of your dog. So often the abominable behavior of an untrained animal irks even those whose interest lies with the breed. Think, then, what a warped impression of the breed must be conveyed, by this same animal, to the critically watching ringsider.

When you enter your Weimaraner in a show, you do so because you believe that he or she is a good enough specimen of the breed to afford competition to, and perhaps win over, the other dogs entered. If your Weimaraner is as good as you think he is, he certainly deserves to be shown to full advantage if you expect him to win or place in this highly competitive sport. A novice handler with a quality Weimaraner that is untrained, unruly, or phlegmatic cannot give competition to a dog of equal, or even lesser, merit which is well trained and handled to full advantage.

Novice owners frequently bring untrained dogs to shows so that they can become accustomed to the strange proceedings and surroundings, hopefully thinking that, in time, the dog will learn to behave in the wanted manner by himself. Often the novice's training for the show ring begins in desperate and intense endeavor within the show ring itself. Confusion for both dog and handler can be the only result of such a program. Preparation for showing must begin long in advance of actual show competition for both dog and handler.

Let us assume that you have been fortunate enough to breed or purchase a puppy who appears to possess all the necessary qualifications for a successful show career. Training for that career should begin from the moment you bring him home, or if you are the breeder, from the time he is weaned. This early training essentially follows the same pattern as does fundamental training in conduct. Again you begin by establishing between you and the puppy the happy relationship which, in time, becomes the control so necessary to all training. Handle the puppy frequently, brush him, examine his teeth, set him up in a show stance, and stroke his back slowly. Move him on a loose

Every year the sport of showing dogs grows in popularity. The Weimaraner is patrunately fortunate in the show ring. This is because there are a large number of good specimens being shown and competition is keen all over the United States. Photo by Louise Van der Meid.

188

To effectively present a dog in the show ring, he should be taught to stand quietly in the position that displays him to best advantage. This training can never start too early in a dog's life. Photo by Louise Van der Meid.

leash, talking to him constantly in a happy, friendly tone. Make all your movements in a deliberate and quiet manner. Praise and pat the puppy often, establishing an easy and happy rapport during this period. This is simple early preparation for the more exact training to come.

During this period the owner and prospective handler should take the opportunity to refresh or broaden his own knowledge. Reread the standard, and with this word picture in mind, build a mental reproduction of the perfect Weimaraner: his structure, balance, gait, and movement. Critically observe the better Weimaraner handlers at shows to see how they set and gait their dogs. Only by accumulating insight and knowledge such as this can you succeed in the training which will bring out the best features of your own future show dog.

Let us assume that your puppy is now old enough to show, or that you have acquired a young dog for whom you plan a show career. Beginning long before the show in which you are going to start him (several weeks at least), you introduce him to the "tidbit." This can be any bit of food which the dog relishes immensely and which is entirely different from the kind of food used in his regular diet. The tidbit, then, is a tasty piece of food which the dog likes and which is not given to him at any other time. Boiled liver, in chunks, is most generally used, but dogs can be shown with liverwurst, peanuts, turkey, or various other treats which the individual animal might particularly relish. If you choose liver as your tidbit, brown it in the oven for a few minutes after you have boiled it. This tends to remove the greasiness from the surface and keeps it from crumbling excessively, making it much easier to handle and carry in your pocket in the show ring. Your pet shop also carries regular training tidbits.

Some dogs are alerted in the show ring by the use of a particular toy, such as a rubber mouse that squeaks when pressed. but many handlers prefer the tidbit. Several times a day when you and your dog are together, tempt him with the tidbit. Always make him stand, never sit, when you offer him this gourmet's delight. Hold the tidbit waist high and allow the dog to smell and taste it. When his complete attention is absorbed in attempting to nibble at this delicious morsel, move slowly backward, carefully watching the dog as he moves forward, until he has taken the proper balanced stance, with his front legs parallel to each other, his back level, and his hind legs stretched back just enough to be comfortable. He is watching the tidbit and posing naturally, alertly, and in proper balance on a loose lead. At this point you, the handler, move forward to within approximately two feet of the dog and command him to "Stand, stay!" Keep his attention focused on the tidbit, speaking gently to him for a few seconds, then give him a small piece of the tidbit as reward and pet and praise him.

Continue this procedure, and, as you progress, make the dog stand motionless and alert for an ever-longer period of time before allowing him to taste the tidbit. When you give him the delicacy as a reward, move forward and present it to him; never allow him to break his pose and come forward to you. Always hold the leash in your left hand. Keep your left leg in front of your right and toward the dog to check him from advancing toward you. If he jumps up for the tidbit, raise your left leg so that your knee takes him in the chest, at the same time jerking strongly downward on the leash.

Next, keeping the leash gathered loosely in your left hand, snug the collar loop high on the dog's neck to smooth away any under-jaw looseness of skin. Hold the leash directly upward and taut to hold his head high. Stand facing the side of the dog and gently place his legs in position. He can be dropped into position in front by lifting him, or the front legs can be placed correctly by hand from the dog's elbow. The hind legs should be handled at the hock

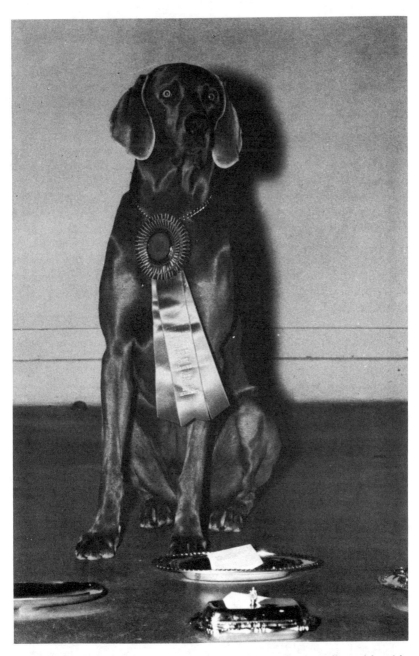

Aquila's Silver Rocket, C.D., owned by John and Lila Bartell, and bred by Mr. Bartell. Sire: Ch. Silver C. Aquila; dam: Silver Prudence. Photo by Henry Schley.

joint when placing. When he is set correctly your right hand is free to attract his attention with the tidbit if necessary. Don't pull to hold him in position, instead use short jerks on the leash. This practice should also be used when moving the dog to keep him in line. When the dog is being examined by the judge, release the front of the dog and move to the back, holding his tail up. Move back to the front, holding your dog in position, as the judge moves toward the animal's hindquarters.

The next step in show training is to teach your dog to move properly when on leash. Weimaraners good enough to be shown generally possess the even, effortless trot which is a distinctive feature of the breed. It is your purpose now to control that beauty of movement so that it loses nothing when displayed in the show ring. Keeping the dog on your left side, move him forward at a slow trot, checking him sharply when he tends to pull out or break stride. Again, the leash should be kept loose. When you come to the end of the allotted run and turn to start back, do not jerk the dog around; instead give him more leash freedom and allow him to come around easily without a change of leads, meanwhile speaking to him quietly. When he has completed the turn, draw him to you with the leash and continue moving back to the starting point. At the finish, pat and praise him.

Although the Weimaraner is a smooth coated dog, some trimming should be done if the dog is to be shown. The muzzle should be cleaned of feelers and superfluous hair. This may be done with scissors or a small electric animal clipper. Photo by Louise Van der Meid.

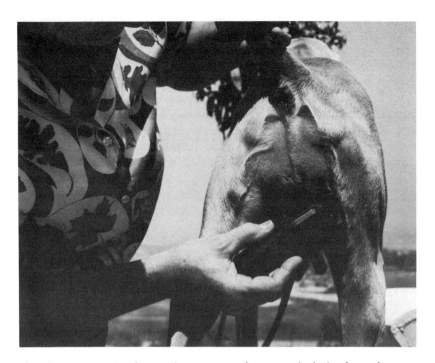

The clipper can also be used to remove the straggly hairs from the rear legs that take away from the smooth outline the Weimaraner should have. Photo by Louise Van der Meid.

While you are teaching your dog the elements of ring deportment, take stock of the pupil himself. To do this correctly, you will need assistance. Have someone else put the dog through his paces, handling him as you have and as he will be handled in the show ring. Observe the dog carefully to determine when he looks his best. Should he be stretched out a bit when posing? Or does he have better balance and outline if his hind legs are not pulled too far back? At what rate of speed, when moving, does he perform his best?

Pretend that you are a judge. Envision the perfect Weimaraner, and employing your knowledge of the standard as a yardstick, study your dog as though he were a strange animal. From this study you will see many things, tiny nuances, that will aid you in showing your Weimaraner to the best possible advantage in open competition.

Once he has mastered the show training you have given him, you must take every opportunity to allow strangers and friends to go over your dog, much in the manner of a judge, while you pose and gait him, so he will become used to a judge's unaccustomed liberties. It would be well to enter your Weimaraner in a few sanction matches now, to acquaint him with the actual condtions under which he will be shown. During all this time, of course, the character and temperament of your dog, as well as his physical assets, must be taken into consideration, as it must in all types of training, and the most made of the best he has.

There is, of course, that paragon of all show dogs, that canine jewel and handler's delight: the alert curious animal who takes a keen interest in the world around him and stands in proud and easy naturalness at the end of his long leash, head and ears up, posing every minute he is in the ring. But remember, even this super-show dog has had some training in ring manners.

In some instances the dog's master stands outside of the ring in full view of his animal while someone else handles him in the ring. The dog will watch his master, keeping his head and ears up and wearing an alert expression. This is called "double-handling," and is sometimes frowned upon by other members of the showing fraternity.

It is of the utmost importance that you never become blind to your dog's faults, but at the same time realize his good features and attempt to exploit these when in the ring. Make sure your dog is in good physical shape, in good coat, clean and well groomed. If a bath is necessary, give it to him several days

Many Weimaraners are shown on the bench and in obedience. This is a great credit to the intelligence and versatility of this fine breed. Photo by Louise Van der Meid.

before the show so the natural oils will have time to smooth the coat and give it a natural sheen. Be sure he is not thirsty when he enters the ring and that he has emptied himself before showing, or it will cramp his movement and make him uncomfortable.

School yourself to be at ease in the ring when handling your dog, for if you are tense and nervous, it will communicate itself to the dog, and he will display the same emotional stress. In the ring, keep one eye on your dog and the other on the judge. One never knows when a judge might turn from the animal he is examining, look at your dog, and perhaps catch him in an awkward moment.

Muzzle whiskers, eyebrows and cheek hairs should be cut close. Also trim any excess hair edges that might mar the smooth silhouette of your Weimaraner from the back of his legs, belly and tail end. If his claws need clipping, tend to it at least four days before show time so that if you should cut too deeply, the claw will have time to heal.

On the morning of the show, leave your home early enough so that you will have plenty of time to be benched and tend to any last minute details which may come up. When the class before yours is in the ring, give your dog a last quick brush, then run a towel over his coat to bring out the gloss. Should his coat be dull, a few drops of brilliantine, rubbed between the palms of your hands and then sparingly applied to the dog's coat, will aid in eliminating the dullness. Some handlers wipe a slightly dampened towel over the coat just before entering the ring to achieve the same effect.

Bring to the show with you: a water pail, towel, brush, comb, suppositories in a small jar, a bench chain, a round leather collar, and a light six-foot slip-collar leash for showing. If the dog has not emptied himself, insert a suppository in his rectum when you take him to the exercising ring. If you forget to bring the suppositories, use instead two paper matches, wet with saliva, from which you have removed the sulphur tips.

In the ring, the handler constantly endeavors to minimize his charge's faults while attempting to inveigle the judge into seeing his virtues. There are several little tricks which the knowing handler employs to accomplish his ends. Should the dog stand east and west in front, the legs must be set correctly by hand. Grasp the dog by the elbow, not the forearm, and gently turn the elbow outward and away from the body until the feet rest parallel to each other. A dog showing lack of rear angulation is offered the tidbit with a pushing motion, while the handler crowds closer to the animal than usual. This causes the dog to sink slightly in the rear quarters, giving the illusion of greater angulation than is actually present. It is good practice with a dog possessing excess vigor to have someone who is not showing take him for a good long run before your class comes up. This will take the edge off his exuberance so he will handle with greater steadiness in the ring, and will not bring the handler into the ring in an exhausted condition.

Chapter XII
Shows and Judging

The basic reason for the dog show, the object in the gathering together of representative animals of the breed in open competition, seems to have been mislaid in the headlong pursuit for ribbons, trophies, and points. These prizes undoubtedly lead to kennel-name popularity, which in turn produces greater and more profitable puppy sales and stud services, but they are not the end in themselves. They are given simply as tokens of achievement in a much larger pattern which has no direct relation to economy. The graded selection of various dogs according to individual quality by a competent, unbiased judge enables earnest breeders to weigh and evaluate the products of certain breedings and strains. It helps them to evaluate their own breeding procedures in relation to comparative quality, and to give them an idea as to which individuals, or breeding lines, can act as correctives to the faults inherent in their own breeding. Here the yardstick of the official standard is used to measure the defects or virtues of individual animals and of the breed as a whole for the edification and tabulation of both the knowing breeder and the novice. This is what a dog show should mean to the exhibitor.

Essentially the judge should be an intermediary between the present and the future, because his decisions shape the trends for better or for worse. If these trends lead to undesirable results, there will be deterioration instead of an ever-closer approach to the breed ideal. The judge is a sounding board, a calculator of degrees of excellence, an instrument for computing worth. He can, with each assignment, give something of enduring value toward breed improvement. As such, he or she must not only be entirely familiar with the Weimaraner standard, but must also understand every element of structure and balance. And almost more important, the judge must be able to see and evaluate each of those tiny nuances of quality which can establish the superiority of one animal over another of apparently equal excellence.

Judges should confine themselves to judging only those breeds with which they have had personal experience. A thorough reading of the standard and the appearance as an apprentice judge does not make anyone an authority on the breed. There should certainly be a more exacting test of ability before

Ch. Bando's Boomerang, owned and bred by H. L. and Mary B. Robinson. Sire: Ch. Bando v.d. Gretchenhof; dam: Ch. Smoky Heritage. Bando is the winner of the parent specialty held with the Harbor Cities Kennel Club. He is shown just after this banner win with his handler, Harry Sangster. Photo by Bennett Associates.

a person is granted a license to judge. We are all conscious of the fact that there are some people who could be in a breed all their lives, read every book published about the breed, and still not qualify as competent judges, simply because they do not possess that special gift that brings clarity and sureness to decision. By the same token, there are perhaps others who do not judge who have that "feel" for a good dog, that gift to select surely which, when combined with knowledge and integrity, makes the completely competent judge.

In the interest of clarity and simplicity, as well as for the edification of the ringsider, a definite pattern of procedure should be adhered to by the judge. All entries in any particular class should be lined up in catalogue order opposite the judge's table. The judge should step into the center of the ring and signal the handlers to circle the ring once or twice, with the dogs maintaining an easy trot. The class should then be halted and the dogs left at rest as the judge calls each dog separately to the center of the ring for individual examination. The judge should approach the dog from the front

Ch. Adandre's Amy, C.D.X., T.D., owned by Dr. and Mrs. H. K. MacHemer and bred by C. A. South. Sire: Ch. Gourmet's Sardar; dam: Ch. Gretchen v. Steed. Photo by Roberts.

Ch. Bonnie's Silver Rocket, N.R.D., owned and bred by Patti A. Long. Sire: Max von Bulverde; dam: Bonnie Blue Belle, II, N.R.D. Photo by Alexander.

and, speaking kindly to him, begin his close examination. Unnecessary handling by the judge is poor practice. There is no reason, other than unsureness by the judge, for bouncing the animal's back like a mattress inspector, pulling the tail up and down, poking here and there as though frisking the dog for dangerous weapons, or any of the other ridiculous actions sometimes indulged in by judges.

After the individual animal has been examined in the center of the ring, the judge should ask to have him gaited at a slow trot, to and away from him, to evaluate movement coming and going. Following this, the dog should be gaited around the ring at a slow trot, to establish his quality in profile movement. When all the animals in the class have been individually examined as described, the entire class should be requested to walk around the ring until the judge has decided upon his placements.

The judge should not only pick his first four dogs, but place the others in the class in the order of their excellence as he sees them. He should know, and, indeed, announce to the handlers of each of the first four dogs placed, the reasons for his selections. Should the judge be unable to explain his placings clearly and concisely, he should refrain from further judging. If this procedure would become an A.K.C. rule, there would undoubtedly be several judges now officiating who would hesitate to accept future assignments. It should also be made mandatory, for the same reasons as mentioned above, for a judge to submit to the A.K.C. a written criticism of all dogs placed by him at any given show.

During the individual examination in the center of the ring, the judge can make notes covering each of the dogs brought before him for future reference. The procedure as outlined above can, of course, be varied to individual taste, but basically it is a standard and sound way of judging.

Though there are times when the judge is at fault, we must not forget that there are many times when the exhibitor's evaluation of the judge's placings is faulty. Too many exhibitors know too little about their own breed and are not competent to indulge in criticism. The very structure of dog-show procedure lends itself to dissatisfaction with the judge's decisions. The fact that there can be only three or fewer really satisfied winners in any

Ch. Kurpfalz Herzogin Hermina, owned and bred by Dr. and Mrs. H. K. MacHemer. Sire: Eilatan's Valstorm Knight; dam: Ch. Adandre's Amy, C.D.X. Photo by Powell.

breed judging, Winner's Male, Winner's Bitch, and Best of Breed, and that they are chosen by one individual who may or may not be competent, leaves a wide range of just or unjust recrimination for the exhibitor to air. Some of the post-mortem denunciation can be attributed directly to the psychological effect of the shows upon the exhibitors themselves.

Almost everyone, at some time or another, has had the urge to engage in some kind of competitive sport. Many exhibitors have arrived at that time of life when most competitive endeavor is too strenuous to be indulged in. Some have been frustrated athletes all their lives due to lack of muscular or physical prowess, or because sustained exertion did not fit their behavior patterns. Nevertheless, the fierce flame of competitiveness burns in them, and the dog-show ring provides a wonderful outlet to satisfy this need of expression. Some, without realizing it, find that the show ring provides an outlet for their normal desire to be important, if even for just a few fleeting moments, and it gives others an opportunity to be on the stage before an audience. The greater number of exhibitors are simply proud of their dogs and want to show them and have them evaluated in competition. Since there is no definite scoring for endeavor, merely a personal evaluation of their animals by an individual who can be right or wrong, tension is built and personalities clash.

The exhibitor has put into the show an enormous amount of time, thought, and heartaches in breeding, rearing, and preparation. With most exhibitors, the very fact that they are present signifies they consider their particular Weimaraner fine enough to win. All this, coupled with some poor judging, often tends to build up strong feelings which sometimes erupt into strong words.

Undoubtedly the whole procedure is of benefit to the exhibitor. He or she indulges in some measure of physical exercise, finds an outlet for the competitive spirit, and presently soothes built-up emotions by letting off vocal steam. But the end result is not good for the breed, since it results in confusion, especially to the novice who comes to the show to learn.

There will always be with us the chronic griper who must tear down another's dog with unfounded criticism after he has been defeated so that his own animal will appear better than it is. We must also deplore the custom of severe criticism and whispering campaigns against a consistent and deserving winner or stud. This insidious undermining of an animal of worth leads the novice to wonder how any judge had the temerity to put him up, which in turn casts reflections upon the judge's ability and further confounds the tyro who is seeking truth.

Many of the most prominent breeders who have been in the breed for years are judges as well. They are frequently criticized for their show-ring placements because they will put up animals of their own breeding or those of similar type to the strain they themselves produce. But in most cases the breeder-judge who elevates animals of his own breeding or dogs of similar type cannot be summarily accused of lack of integrity. The type which he breeds must be the type of animal he likes and his own interpretation of the standard. It follows, therefore, that this is the type he will put up in all honesty. We may question his taste, knowledge, or interpretation of the standard, but not, in most instances, his ethics or honesty.

Undeniably, there are many instances in which a dog, handled or owned by an individual who is himself a judge, is given preference, since the breeder-judge officiating at the moment will, in the near future, show under the owner of the dog he has put up and expects the same consideration in return This is but one of the many ways in which a judge may be influenced consciously or unconsciously. Regardless of the underlying cause, such practice must be condemned.

It is true that some judges seem to develop special prejudices on particular points of structure. For this reason it might have been wise to have included a numerical evaluation of points in the standard to check any tendency by a judge to overemphasize some minor fault which he particularly detests. Still, in some instances, this emphasis can be a boon, causing quick elimination of some fault which, if allowed to become concentrated, could become a definite menace to the perfection we strive for. When such a condition does exist, the judges of the breed should be made aware of this tendency and, by penalizing it in the ring and vocally stressing this fact in evaluating the animal to its handler, do their share toward its elimination.

We are frequently told that the element of human variance in the interpretation of the standard is responsible for the wide difference of placings from one show to the next. Certainly this is true, but it should only be true to a limited extent. A judge's interpretation of the standard and his knowledge of what is a fault or a credit cannot vary so greatly from show to show if dictated alone by the human equation. Acknowledging the slight variance in placing which the individual judge's interpretation might cause, there is still no excuse for the wide discrepancy, and sometimes weird difference in placings, which we see occur too frequently. When we see this type of bad or biased judging, we can only assume that the arbitrator is either dishonest or ignorant and, in either case, is doing the breed great harm.

There are, thank goodness, quite a few qualified and earnest judges whose placings should be followed and analyzed, for it is through them that we can evaluate the breeding health of the Weimaraner and know with confidence the individual worth of specific specimens. Judging is not an easy task. It does not generally lead to long and cozy friendships, for once an individual steps into the ring to begin his judiciary assignment, he is no longer an individual but becomes the impartial, wholly objective instrument of the standard. As such, friendship and personal likes or dislikes cannot exist as facets of his make-up. He must judge the dogs before him as they are on that day without sentiment or favor. This is a task that demands complete subjection of self, high knowledge of the breed, and courage and integrity. It can be easily seen then, that not too many people could qualify in all these respects and so become completely proficient judges.

The judging situation must be improved. A system should be set up whereby only those who have passed some rigid test would be qualified to judge the breed. As it exists today, instead of a process of selection tending toward breed improvement, we have nothing but unsureness leading to chaos. Were the ideal condition to exist, we, the breeders and owners, would submit our animals in open competition to the careful scrutiny of a truly competent authority whose integrity was beyond question. We would be able to compare our stock within the ring to see where we had erred. We would be able to measure the worth of breeding theory by the yardstick of a correct interpretation of the standard. We would know then what breeding lines were producing animals closest to the ideal and which individual dogs showed the highest degree of excellence; by thus creating, through the medium of the judge, an authority which we could depend upon, we could establish an easier path to the breed ideal.

Following is a chart listing the dog-show classes and indicating eligibility in each class, with appropriate remarks. This chart will tell you at a glance which is the best class for your dog.

DOG-SHOW CLASS CHART

CLASS	ELIGIBLE DOGS	REMARKS
PUPPY—6 months and under 9 months	All puppies from 6 months up to 9 months.	
PUPPY—9 months and under 12 months	All puppies from 9 months to 12 months.	
NOVICE	Any dog or puppy which has not won an adult class (over 12 months), or any higher award, at a point show.	After three first-place Novice wins, cannot be shown again in the class.
BRED BY EXHIBITOR	Any dog or puppy, other than a Champion, which is owned and bred by exhibitor.	Must be shown only by a member of immediate family of breeder-exhibitor, i.e., husband, wife, father, mother, son, daughter, brother, sister.

AMERICAN-BRED	All dogs or puppies whelped in the U.S. or possessions, except Champions.	
OPEN DOGS	All dogs, 6 months of age or over, including Champions and foreign-breds.	Canadian and foreign champions are shown in open until acquisition of American title. By common courtesy, most American Champions are entered only in Specials.
SPECIALS CLASS	American Champions	Compete for B.O.B., for which no points are given.

Each sex is judged separately. The winners of each class compete against each other for Winners (first place) and Reserve Winners (second place). The animal designated as Winners is awarded points. Reserve Winners receive no points. Reserve Winners can be the second dog in the class from which the Winners Dog was chosen. The Winners Male and Winners Female (Winners Dog and Winners Bitch) compete for Best of Winners. The one chosen Best of Winners competes against the Specials for Best of Breed, and the Best of Breed winner goes into the Group. If fortunate enough to top the Group, the final step is to compete against the other group winners for the Best in Show title.

When Best of Breed is awarded, Best of Opposite Sex is also chosen. A Weimaraner which has taken the points in its own sex as Winners, yet has been defeated for Best of Winners, can still be awarded Best of Opposite Sex if there are no animals of its sex appearing in the ring for the Best of Breed award.

Champions are made by the point system. Only the Winners Dog and Winners Bitch receive points, and the number of points won depends upon the number of Weimaraners of its own sex the dog has defeated in the classes (not by the number entered). The United States is divided into five regional point groups by the A.K.C., and the point rating varies with the region in which the show is held. Consult a show catalogue for regional rating. A Weimaraner going Best of Winners is allowed the same number of points as the animal of the opposite sex which it defeats if the points are of a greater number than it won by defeating members of its own sex. No points are awarded for Best of Breed.

To become a Champion, a dog must win fifteen points under a minimum of three different judges. In accumulating these points, the dog must win points in at least two major (three points or more) shows, under different judges. Five points is the maximum amount that can be won at any given

Ch. Chan of Taunus, owned by Ann DeEspinosa and bred by Hubert J. and Virginia L. Long. Chan is shown winning the national specialty. The judge of this show was Alva Rosenberg. This fine male was handled to this important win by Jack Funk, with whom he is pictured. Photo by Ritter.

show. If your Weimaraner wins a group, he is entitled to the highest number of points won in any of the sporting breeds by the dogs he defeats in the group if the points exceed the amount he has won in his own breed. If the show is a Weimaraner Specialty, then the Best of Breed winner automatically becomes the Best in Show dog. No points are awarded at Match or Sanctioned shows. Incidentally, for the good of the breed, it should be every judge's stern duty ruthlessly to eliminate from show ring competition any animal which shows major faults of temperament.

Remember that showing dogs is a sport, not a matter of life and death, so take your lickings with the same smile that you take your winnings, even if it hurts (and it does). Tomorrow is another day, another show, another judge. The path of the show dog is never strewn with roses, though it may look that way to the novice handler who seems, inevitably, to step on thorns. Always be a good sport, don't run the other fellow's dog down because he has beaten yours, and when a Weimaraner goes into the group, give him your hearty applause even if you don't like the dog, his handler, his owner, and his breeding. Remember only that he is a Weimaraner, a representative of your breed and therefore the best darn dog in the group.

Chapter XIII
Basic Field Training

The first and most important essential to gun dog training, coupled with control, is a perfect understanding between dog and owner. This rapport must be established early so that your Weimaraner puppy has complete confidence in you, his master. Once this has been achieved you will always have your dog's eager attention, and he will leap to obey your commands of voice, whistle, or hand signal.

Your dog's general training will come in handy now. You can teach your pupil to sit at a whistled command instead of a verbal one. The instruction he has been given will be extremely useful in the field, and all the many commands you have taught him to obey in the process of molding him into a proper house dog and companion will augment his field training.

Perhaps the most important general trait we must make sure of in the gun dog is his steadiness to sharp sounds, for a gun shy dog is the epitome of uselessness in the field. Early training, the earlier the better, is the key to a gunsure dog. If you have bred the litter yourself, and your bitch (the dam) is definitely not gun shy, you can begin making the puppies sound-sure during the weaning period. While the hungry little puppies are gobbling up their food, fire pistol shots into the air at intervals, and at a short distance from the puppies. If they show no sign of disturbance from the sharp reports, change to a rifle and later a shotgun, firing when they are engrossed in their food. The steadiness of the mother bitch also acts as an example to the puppies.

The same procedure can be followed if you have bought a Weimaraner puppy. But, in this case, first allow the youngster time to settle in, to be at home and confident in his new environment. Then, when the hungry puppy is happily eating, fire a gun. An alternate time to begin training for gunsureness would be when the puppy is completely engrossed in happy play with someone in the family with whom he has fallen deeply in love, usually a youngster. The puppy's playmate must be warned, of course, to evince no reaction to the sound of the gun.

Puppies love to chase and retrieve a thrown object. The big trouble here is that it is more play than serious work for them to retrieve the dummy. In teaching to retrieve you make the puppy sit until given the command to fetch.

Gerri's Fresno Rowdy, owned by John B. Ducato, and bred by I. W. Steward. Sire: Field Ch. Gerri v. Fabien; dam: Sue of Beacon Hill. Rowdy is a classic example of the Weimaraner's great stylishness in the field, and intensity on point. The distinctive beauty of the hunting Weimaraner is responsible, to a great degree for the breed's current popularity. Photo by John Ducato.

The sit period is gradually lengthened until the dog realizes that the fetch is to be made only upon command.

Do not make your puppy work too long, and vary his work often so that he will not be driven to lackadaisical conduct through boredom engendered by repeating the same set of exercises for too long a period during any one training session.

Here again the earlier deportment training can be useful, for, by utilizing it, many more and varied exercises can be indulged in to keep your puppy alert and eager.

Patience is a necessary virtue that must be developed by the trainer. Some puppies take much more time to develop than others. There is, today, due to the many field trials throughout the country, a tendency to push, to try to develop the young dog fast so that he can be entered in trials. This can ruin a good dog that is a slow developer. Many professional trainers forget that field trial dogs are asked to do much more than they were a few years ago. They are obsessed with the idea that there is no limit to what a dog can and should do,

Patience on the part of the trainer and care for the education of the dog in the field, will result in a gunning companion that will understand his job perfectly, and prove a pleasure to shoot over. Photo by Louise Van der Meid.

Field Ch. Smoker Rooney, owned by Mrs. Susan G. Hannum, and bred by Donald C. Davis. Sire: Chester's Silver Love; dam: Silver Jessie Bell. Photo by Lewis Craig.

regardless of the shortness of the training period. The result is a few very good dogs and many mediocre animals that could have been excellent field dogs if given more time to develop and learn.

The puppy that is slow to develop, who shows no desire or interest in his work, cannot be forced. It is best to work this type of puppy with an older dog. Frequently the youngster's interest will be aroused and he will begin to imitate. Keep the puppy with you as much as possible so that he can watch and, you hope, eventually become aware of his responsibility to you and his heritage.

Sometimes a puppy who has been doing beautifully will suddenly seem to lose interest in the whole proceeding. Don't try to force him. Instead, give him a short vacation from all training. Generally, when you bring him out again, he will go to work with zest and vigor and grasp new lessons with greater rapidity than before.

Dogs, like children, must be chastised immediately when they do wrong. You will generally find that your Weimaraner puppy is sensitive enough to be hurt by verbal scolding and the sharpness in your voiced displeasure. Occasionally, you have to deal with the stubborn, insensitive dog who can stand a thrashing without undue mental disturbance. But many dogs have been spoiled by the wrong kind and intensity of chastisement. Only scold or chastise the puppy when he can be caught in the act of disobeying. For example, if your puppy breaks before command and retrieves the object and delivers it to you, he should not be punished, for he will think he is being punished for retrieving and returning the retrieve to hand. Catch him as he breaks before the command and before he reaches the object to be retrieved. Scold him and make him obey until relieved by your command to make the retrieve.

Most of all, remember never to lose your temper. All chastisement must be done methodically and coldly and never in anger.

Puppies, during the early training period, will sometimes exhibit varied and exasperating traits and habits. Most of these will disappear with experience and, by indulging in restraint and patience, the trainer will usually find that the puppy will correct himself and lose his early mischieveousness.

In Germany, the Weimaraner was used on furred as well as feathered game. American sportsmen have put his talents to work mainly on birds; the result is a dog of flawless performance and great skill in all phases of hunting. Photo by Louise Van der Meid.

Double dummy retrieves often take the dog a bit of time to learn. Just be sure that each lesson is learned and executed with efficiency before going on to the next one.

Use the whistle as a call and this will teach your Weimaraner to quickly respond. For the recall use a long blast followed quickly by two short ones. Use this recall signal to call your dog to you in the initial training. A single whistle blast is the "stop" and the "sit" signal. The recall can, and should, be used in very early training, to call the puppy to his meals and when out walking to call him in when you change direction.

In the field the recall is used to bring your dog all the way in, or to bring him in closer until he reaches a point where you wish to stop him and send him in another direction.

The whistle is also the means by which you get your dog's attention so that you can direct him with hand signals. Never send your dog to a spot where there is nothing to find, even during training. He will remember and lose his sharpness while working.

Don't overdo whistle and hand directions or you will develop a mechanical hunter. Instead allow your dog to use his nose and his inherited ability in the field so that he will seek and find game by himself and make his work in the field a greater pleasure to both himself and you, his master.

Remember, too, to constantly and with conviction and enthusiasm, praise your dog when he performs correctly. Let him know that you are pleased for this, from you, the one he loves, means more to the dog than any other pleasure on earth.

Only the initial training essentials are outlined here. For advanced training, trailing, correcting hard mouth and retrieving mistakes, retrieving dead and live game, water work, detailed and more complicated directional signals, steadiness to wing and shot, and the many tricks and intricacies employed by professional trainers for specific correction and finish, there are many good books written especially for gun dog training. Valuable and much more complete information is available in such books than can be found here in a book dealing with all the myriad facets of a specific breed.

Just remember that your Weimaraner was developed as a sporting breed. To keep him only as a pet and deny him the privilege of his heritage as a gun dog in the field, is to steal from him a major part of his reason for being, to deny him the joy of doing that which he does best. And it denies you, his owner, the rare and heart-warming pleasure of watching your "Gray Ghost" in all his specific glory, working, floating across a field, doing what comes naturally to a Weimaraner.

Chapter XIV
Diseases and First Aid

The dog is heir to many illnesses, and, as with man, it seems that when one dread form has been overcome by some specific medical cure, another quite as lethal takes its place. It is held by some that this cycle will always continue, since it is nature's basic way of controlling species population.

There are, of course, several ways to circumvent Dame Nature's lethal plans. The initial step in this direction is to put the health of your dogs in the hands of one who has the knowledge and equipment, mental and physical, to competently cope with your canine health problems. We mean, of course, a modern veterinarian. Behind this man are years of study and experience and a knowledge of all the vast research, past and present, which has developed the remarkable cures and artificial immunities that have so drastically lowered the canine mortality rate as of today.

Put your trust in the qualified veterinarian and "beware of Greeks bearing gifts." Beware, too, of helpful friends who say, "I know what the trouble is and how to cure it. The same thing happened to my dog." Home doctoring by unskilled individuals acting upon the advice of unqualified "experts" has killed more dogs than distemper.

Your Weimaraner is constantly exposed to innumerable diseases through the medium of flying and jumping insects, helminths, bacteria, fungi, and viruses. His body develops defenses and immunities against many of these diseases, but there are many more which we must cure or immunize him against if they are not to prove fatal.

We are not qualified to give advice about treatment for the many menaces to your dog's health that exist and, by the same token, you are not qualified to treat your dog for these illnesses with the skill or knowledge necessary for success. We can only give you a resumé of modern findings on the most prevalent diseases and illnesses so that you can, in some instances, eliminate them or the causative agent yourself. Even more important, this chapter will help you recognize their symptoms in time to seek the aid of your veterinarian.

Though your dog can contract disease at any time or any place, he or she is most greatly exposed to danger when in the company of other dogs at field trials and dog shows or in a boarding kennel. Watch your dog carefully after it has been hospitalized or sent afield to be bred. Many illnesses have an incubation period, during the early stages of which the animal himself may not show the symptoms of the disease, but can readily contaminate other dogs with which he comes in contact. It is readily seen, then, that places where many dogs are gathered together, such as those mentioned above, are particularly dangerous to your dog's health.

Parasitic diseases, which we will first investigate, must not be taken too lightly, though they are the easiest of the diseases to cure. Great suffering and even death can come to your dog through these parasites that prey on him if you neglect to realize the importance of both cure and the control of reinfestation.

EXTERNAL PARASITES

The lowly flea is one of the most dangerous insects from which you must protect your dog. It carries and spreads tapeworm, heartworm and bubonic plague, causes loss of coat and weight, spreads skin disease, and brings untold misery to its poor host. These pests are particularly difficult to combat because their eggs—of which they lay thousands—can lie dormant for months, hatching when conditions of moisture and warmth are present. Thus you may think you have rid your dog (and your house) of these devils, only to find that they mysteriously reappear as weather conditions change.

When your dog has fleas, use any good commerical flea powder that contains malathion, lindane, or any similar insecticide. Pyrethrins and rotenone flea powders are excellent, but not long lasting. Dust him freely with the powder. It is not necessary to cover the dog completely, since the flea is active and will quickly reach a spot saturated with the powder and die. These compounds are also fatal to lice. DDT in liquid soap is excellent and long-potent, its effects lasting for as long as a week. Your dog's sleeping quarters as well as the animal itself should be treated. Repeat the treatment in ten days to eliminate fleas which have been newly hatched from dormant eggs. Chlorinated hydrocarbons (DDT, chlordane, dieldrin, etc.) are long acting. Organic phosphoriferous substances such as malathion, are quick killers with no lasting effect.

TICKS

There are many kinds of ticks, all of which go through similar stages in their life process. At some stage in their lives they all find it necessary to feed on blood. Luckily, these vampires are fairly easily controlled. The female of the species is much larger than the male, which will generally be found hiding under the female. Care must be taken in the removal of these pests to guard against the head's remaining embedded in the dog's skin when the body of the tick is removed. Chlorinated hydrocarbons are effective tick removers. Ether or nail-polish remover, touched to the individual tick, will cause it to relax its grip and fall off the host. The heated head of a match from which the flame has been just extinguished, employed in the same fashion, will cause individual ticks to release their hold and fall from the dog. After veterinary tick treatment, no attempt should be made to remove the pests manually, since the treatment will cause them to drop by themselves as they succumb.

MITES

There are three basic species of mites that generally infect dogs, the demodectic mange mite (red mange), the sarcoptic mange mite (white mange), and the ear mite (otodectic mange). Demodectic mange is generally recognized by balding areas on the face, cheeks, and the front parts of the foreleg, which present a moth-eaten appearance. Reddening of the skin and great irritation occurs as a result of the frantic rubbing and scratching of affected parts by the animal. Rawness and thickening of the skin follows. Not too long ago this was a dread disease in dogs, from which few recovered. It is still a persistent and not easily cured condition unless promptly diagnosed and diligently attended to.

Sarcoptic mange mites can infest you as well as your dog. The resulting disease is known as scabies. This disease very much resembles dry dermatitis, or what is commonly called "dry eczema." The coat falls out and the denuded area becomes inflamed and itches constantly.

Ear mites, of course, infest the dog's ear and can be detected by an accumulation of crumbly dark brown or black wax within the ear. Shaking of the head and frequent scratching at the site of the infestation accompanied by squeals and grunting also is symptomatic of the presence of these pests. Canker of the ear is a condition, rather than a specific disease, which covers a wide range of ear infection. Canker can be initiated by ear mite infection.

All three of these conditions should be treated by your veterinarian. By taking skin scrapings or wax particles from the ear for microscopic examination, he can make an exact diagnosis and recommend specific treatment. The irritations caused by these ailments, unless immediately controlled, can result in loss of appetite and weight, and so lower your dog's natural resistance that he is open to the attack of other diseases which his bodily defenses could normally battle successfully.

INTERNAL PARASITES

It seems strange, in the light of new discovery of specific controls for parasitism, that the incidence of parasitic infestation should still be almost as

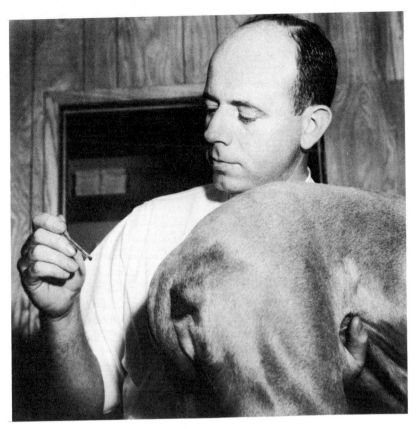

A dog's temperature is normally higher than that of a human being. Your veterinarian can show you how to take temperature and how to determine whether or not your dog has a fever. Photo by Louise Van der Meid.

great as it was years ago. This can only be due to lack of realization by the dog owner of the importance of initial prevention and control against reinfestation. Strict hygiene must be adhered to if dogs properly treated are not to be exposed to infestation immediately again. This is particularly true where worms are concerned.

In attempting to rid our dogs of worms, we must not be swayed by amateur opinion. The so-called "symptoms" of worms may be due to many other reasons. We may see the actual culprits in the animal's stool, but even then it is not wise to worm indiscriminately. The safest method to pursue is to take a small sample of your dog's stool to your veterinarian. By a fecal analysis he can advise just what specific types of worms infest your dog and what drugs should be used to eliminate them.

215

Do not worm your dog because you "think" he should be wormed, or because you are advised to do so by some self-confessed "authority." Drugs employed to expel worms can prove highly dangerous to your dog if used indiscriminately and carelessly, and in many instances the same symptoms that are indicative of the presence of internal parasites can also be the signs of some other affliction.

A word here in regard to that belief that garlic will "cure" worms. Garlic is an excellent flavoring agent, favored by gourmets the world over, but it will not rid your dog of worms. Its only curative power lies in the fact that, should you use it on a housedog who has worms, the first time he pants in your face you will definitely be cured of ever attempting this psuedo-remedy again.

ROUNDWORM

These are the most common worms found in dogs and can have grave effects upon puppies, which they almost invariably infest. Potbellies, general unthriftiness, diarrhea, coughing, lack of appetite, anemia, are the symptoms. They can also cause verminous pneumonia when in the larval stage. Fecal examinations of puppy stools should be made by your veterinarian frequently if control of these parasites is to be constant. Although theoretically it is possible for small puppies to be naturally worm free, actually most puppies are born infested (larvae in the bloodstream of the bitch cross the placenta to infect the unborn pups) or contract the eggs at the mother's breast or from the surrounding environment.

The roundworm lives in the intestine and feeds on the dog's partially digested food, growing and laying eggs which are passed out in the dog's stool to be picked up by him in various ways and so cause reinfestation. The life history of all the intestinal worms is a vicious circle, with the dog the beginning and the end host. This worm is yellowish-white in color and is shaped like a common garden worm, pointed at both ends. It is usually curled when found in the stool. There are several different species of this type of worm. Some varieties are more dangerous than others. They discharge toxin within the dog, and the presence of larvae in important organs of the dog's body can cause death.

The drugs most used by kennel owners for the elimination of roundworms are N-butyl-chloride, tetrachloroethylene and the piperazines, but there are a host of other drugs, new and old, that can also do the job efficiently. With most of the worm drugs, give no food to the dog for twenty-four hours, or in the case of puppies, twenty hours, previous to the time he is given the medicine. It is absolutely essential that this starvation limit be adhered to if the drug used is tetrachloroethylene, since the existence of the slightest amount of food in the stomach or intestine can cause death. One tenth c.c.

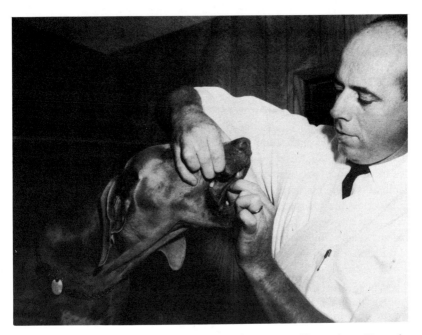

Giving a dog a pill or capsule is a simple matter. Place the pill as far back on the dog's tongue as possible. Close the mouth and hold the head up. Then stroke the dog's throat until the dog swallows the pill. Photo by Louise Van der Meid.

to each pound of the animal's weight up to 50 pounds is the dosage for tetrachloroethylene, followed in one hour with a milk-of-magnesia physic, never an oily physic. Food may be given two hours later. Piperazines are less toxic, and the dog can be fed normally. Large doses of the drug can be given grown dogs without danger.

HOOKWORMS

These tiny worms that live on the blood of your dog, which they get from the intestinal walls, cause severe anemia, groaning, fits, diarrhea, loss of appetite and weight, rapid breathing, and swelling of the legs. Some of the same drugs used to eradicate roundworms will also expel hookworms. Disophenol, in subcutaneous injection, is the newest and most effective hook-work treatment. Tetrachlorethylene, n-butyl-chloride and tolkuene are drugs also used for hookworms.

Good food is essential for quick recovery, with added amounts of liver and raw meat and iron tonics incorporated in the diet. Blood transfusions are often necessary if the infestation has been heavy. If one infestation follows another, a certain degree of immunity to the effects of the parasite seems to be built up by the dog. A second treatment should be given two weeks following the initial treatment.

WHIPWORMS

These small, thin whiplike worms are found in the intestines and the cecum. Those found in the intestines are reached and killed by the same drugs used in the eradication of roundworms and hookworms. Most worm medicines will kill these helminths if they reach them, but those which live in the cecum are very difficult to reach. They exude toxins which cause debilitation, anemia, and allied ills, and are probably a contributing factor in lowering the resistance to the onslaught of other infections. The usual symptoms of worm infestation are present, especially vomiting, diarrhea, and loss of weight. Phthalofyne is an effective whipworm eradicator. It can be administered by either intravenous injection or by oral tablets.

The Weimaraner that is used in the hunting field should be checked after every expedition for cuts, bruises, and parasites. If this important procedure is overlooked, serious difficulties can result. Photo by Louise Van der Meid.

TAPEWORMS

Tapeworms are not easily diagnosed by fecal test, but are easily identified when visible in the dog's stool. The worm is composed of two distinct parts, the head and the segmented body. It is pieces of the segmented body that we see in the stools of the dog. They are usually pink or white in color and flat. The common tapeworm, which is most prevalent in our dogs, is about eighteen inches long, and the larvae are carried by the flea. The head of the worm is smaller than a pinhead and attaches itself to the intestinal wall. Contrary to general belief, the dog infested with tapeworms does not possess an enormous appetite, rather it fluctuates from good to poor. The animal shows the general signs of worm infestation. Often he squats and drags his hindquarters on the ground. This is due to tapeworm segments moving and wriggling in the lower bowels. One must be careful in diagnosing this symptom, as it may also mean that the dog is suffering from distended anal glands.

Arecolene is one of the most efficient expellers of tapeworms. Dosage is approximately one-tenth grain for every fifteen pounds of the dog's weight, administered after twenty hours of fasting. No worm medicine can be considered 100 percent effective in all cases. If one drug does not expel the worms satisfactorily, then another must be tried.

HEARTWORM

This villain inhabits the heart and is the most difficult to treat. The worm is about a foot long and literally stuffs the heart of the affected animal. It is prevalent in the southern states and has long been the curse of sporting-dog breeds. This does not signify that other dogs cannot become infected, since the worm is transmitted principally through the bite of an infected mosquito, which can fly from an infected southern canine visitor directly to another dog and do its dire deed.

The symptoms are: fatigue, gasping, coughing, nervousness, and sometimes dropsy and swelling of the extremities. Treatment for heartworms definitely must be left in the hands of your veterinarian. A wide variety of drugs are used in treatment, the most commonly employed are the arsenicals, antimony compounds, and caracide. Danger exists during cure when dying worms move to the lungs, causing suffocation, or when dead worms, in a heavily infested dog, block the small blood vessels in the heart muscles. The invading microfilariae are not discernible in the blood until nine months following introduction of the disease by the bite of the carrier mosquito.

In an article on this subject in *Field and Stream* magazine, Joe Stetson describes a controlled experiment in which caracide was employed in periodic treatments as a preventive of heartworm. The experiment was carried out over a period of eighteen months, during which time the untreated dogs became positive for heartworm and eventually died. A post mortem proved the presence of the worm. The dogs that underwent scheduled prophylaxis have been found, by blood test, to be free of circulating microfilariae and are thriving.

COCCIDIOSIS

This disease is caused by a tiny protozoan. It affects dogs of all ages, but is not dangerous to mature animals. When puppies become infected by a severe case of coccidiosis, it very often proves fatal, since it produces such general weakness and emaciation that the puppy has no defense against other invading harmful organisms. Loose and bloody stools are indicative of the presence of this disease, as is loss of appetite, weakness, emaciation, discharge from the eyes, and a fever of approximately 103 degrees. The disease is contracted directly or through flies that have come from infected quarters. Infection seems to occur over and over again, limiting the puppy's chance of recovery with each succeeding infection. The duration of the disease is about three weeks, but new infestations can stretch this period of illness on until your

To administer liquid medicine, the corner of the dog's lip should be pulled back and the medicine allowed to run down the pouch thus formed. Photo by Louise Van der Meid.

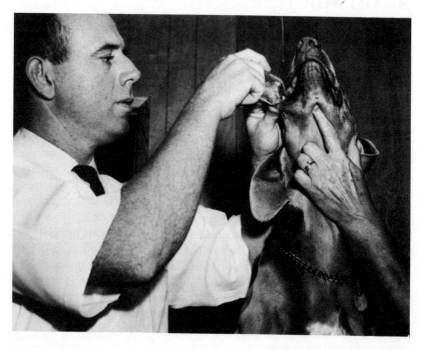

puppy has little chance to recover. Strict sanitation and supportive treatment of good nutrition—utilizing milk, fat, kaopectate, and bone ash (a tablespoonful a day for Weimaraner puppies), with added dextrose and calcium—seem to be all that can be done in the way of treatment. Force feed the puppy if necessary. The more food that you can get into him to give him strength until the disease has run its course, the better will be his chances of recovery. Specific cures have been developed in other animals and poultry, but not as yet in dogs. Fragmentary clinical evidence would seem to indicate that sulfamethazine may give some control in canine coccidiosis.

SKIN DISEASES

Diseases of the skin in dogs are many, varied, and easily confused by the kennel owner as to category. All skin afflictions should be immediately diagnosed by your veterinarian so that treatment can begin with dispatch. Whatever drug is prescribed must be employed diligently and in quantity and generally long after surface indications of the disease have ceased to exist. A surface cure may be attained, but the infection remains buried deep in the hair follicles or skin glands, to erupt again if treatment is suspended too soon. Contrary to popular belief, diet, if well balanced and complete, is seldom the cause of skin disease.

Eczema

The word "eczema" is a much-abused word, as is the word "dermatitis." Both are used with extravagance in the identification of various forms of skin disorders. We will concern ourselves with the two most prevalent forms of so-called eczema, namely wet eczema and dry eczema, In the wet form, the skin exudes moisture and then scabs over, due to constant scratching and biting by the dog at the site of infection. The dry form manifests itself in dry patches which irritate and itch, causing great discomfort to the dog. In both instances the hair falls out and the spread of the disease is rapid. The cause of these diseases is not yet known, though many are thought to be originated by various fungi and bacteria and aggravated by flea allergic conditions and self trauma. The quickest means of bringing these diseases under control is through the application of a good skin remedy often combined with a fungicide, which your veterinarian will prescribe. An over-all dip, employing specific liquid medication, is beneficial in many cases and has a continuing curative effect over a period of days. Injectable or oral anti-inflammatory drugs are often employed as supplementary treatment.

Ringworm

This infection is caused by a fungus and is highly contagious to humans. In the dog it generally appears on the face as a round or oval spot from which the hair has fallen. It is not as often seen in long-coated dogs as it is in shorter-coated dogs. Ringworm is easily controlled by the application of iodine glycerine (fifty percent of each ingredient) or a fungicide such as girseofulvin, a definite cure for ringworm.

Acne

Your puppy will frequently display small eruptions on his belly or eyelids, paws and muzzle. The rash is caused by a bacterial infection of the skin glands and hair follicles and is not serious if treated early. Wash the affected areas with alcohol or witch hazel and apply a healing lotion or powder. Hormonal imbalances can cause specific skin conditions that are best left to the administrations of your veterinarian.

Hookworm Larvae Infection

The skin of your dog can become infected from the larvae of the hookworm acquired from muddy hookworm-infested runs. The larvae become stuck to his coat with mud and burrow into the skin, leaving ugly raw red patches. One or two baths in warm water to which an antiseptic has been added usually cures the condition quickly.

DEFICIENCY DISEASES

These diseases, or conditions, are caused by dietary deficiencies or some condition which robs the diet of necessary ingredients. Anemia, a deficiency condition, is a shortage of hemoglobin. Hookworms, lice, and any disease that depletes the system of red blood cells, are contributory causes. A shortage or lack of specific minerals or vitamins in the diet can also cause anemia Not so long ago, rickets was the most common of the deficiency diseases, caused by a lack of one or more of the dietary elements: vitamin D, calcium, and phosphorous. There are other types of deficiency diseases originating in dietary inadequacy and characterized by unthriftiness in one or more phases. The cure exists in supplying the missing food factors to the diet. Sometimes, even though all the necessary dietary elements are present in the food, some are destroyed by improper feeding procedure. For example, a substance in raw eggs, avertin, destroys biotin, one of the B-complex group of vitamins. Cooking will destroy the avertin in the egg white and prevent a biotin deficiency in the diet.

BACTERIAL DISEASES

In this group we find leptospirosis, tetanus, pneumonia, and many other dangerous diseases. The mortality rate is generally high in all of the bacterial diseases, and treatment should be left to your veterinarian.

Leptospirosis

Leptospirosis is spread most frequently by the urine of infected dogs, which can infect for six months or more after the animal has recovered from the disease. Rats are the carriers of the bacterial agent that produces this disease. A dog will find a bone upon which an infected rat has urinated, chew the bone, and become infected with the disease in turn. Leptospirosis is primarily dangerous in the damage it does to the kidneys. Complete isolation of affected individuals to keep the disease from spreading and rat control of kennel areas are the chief means of control. Vaccines are employed by your veterinarian as a preventive measure. Initial diagnosis is difficult, and the disease generally makes drastic inroads before a cure is effected. It has been estimated that fully fifty percent of all dogs throughout the world have been stricken with leptospirosis at one time or another, and that in many instances the disease was not recognized for what it was. The disease produced by *Leptospira* in the blood of humans is known as Weil's disease.

Tetanus

Lockjaw bacteria produce an exceedingly deadly poison. The germs grow in the depths of a sealed-over wound where oxygen cannot penetrate. To prevent this disease, every deep wound acquired by your dog should be thoroughly cleansed and disinfected, and an antitoxin given the animal. Treatment follows the same general pattern as prevention. If the jaw locks, intravenous feeding must be given.

Tonsillitis

Inflammation of the tonsils can be either of bacterial or virus origin. It is not a serious disease in itself, but is often a symptom of other diseases. The symptoms of tonsillitis are enlarged and reddened tonsils, poor appetite, vomiting, and optic discharge. The condition usually runs its course in from five to seven days. Penicillin, aureomycin, terramycin, chloromycetin, etc., have been used with success in treatment.

Pneumonia

Pneumonia is a bacterial disease of the lungs of which the symptoms are poor appetite, optic discharge, shallow and rapid respiration. Affected animals become immune to the particular type of pneumonia from which they have recovered. Oral treatment utilizing antibiotic or sulfa drugs, combined with a pneumonia jacket of cloth or cotton padding wrapped around the chest area, seems to be standard treatment. Pneumonia is quite often associated with distemper.

VIRAL DISEASES

The dread viral diseases are caused by the smallest organisms known to man. They live in the cells and often attack the nerve tissue. The tissue thus weakened is easily invaded by many types of bacteria. Complications then set in, and it is these accompanying ills which usually prove fatal. The secondary infections can be treated with several of the "wonder" drugs, and excellent care and nursing is necessary if the stricken animal is to survive. Your veterinarian is the only person qualified to aid your dog when a virus disease strikes. The diseases in this category include distemper, infectious hepatitis, rabies, kennel cough, and primary encephalitis—the latter actually inflammation of the brain, a condition characterizing several illnesses, particularly those of viral origin.

Distemper

Until recently a great many separate diseases had been lumped under the general heading of distemper.* In the last few years modern science has isolated a number of separate diseases of the distemper complex. Thus, with more accurate diagnosis, great strides have been made in conquering, not only distemper, but these other, allied diseases. Distemper (Carre) is no longer prevalent due to successful methods of immunization, but any signs of illness in an animal not immunized may be the beginning of the disease.

Modern veterinary medicine has perfected many serums that render the dreaded canine diseases of the past almost completely controllable. Photo by Louise Van der Meid.

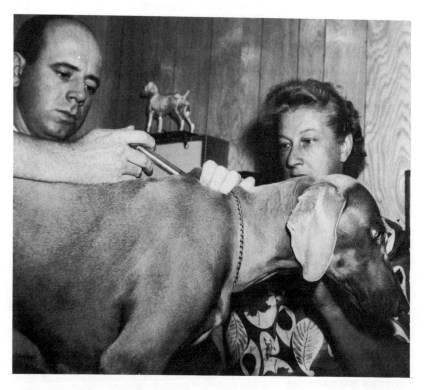

* See L. F. and G. D. Whitney, *The Distemper Complex* (Orange, Conn., Practical Science Publishing Co., 1953).

The symptoms are so similar to those of various other diseases that only a trained observer can diagnose correctly. Treatment consists of the use of drugs to counteract complications arising from the invasion of secondary diseases and in keeping the stricken animal warm, well fed, comfortable and free from dehydration until the disease has run its course. In many instances, even if the dog gets well, he will be left with some dreadful souvenir of the disease which will mar him for life.

The tremendous value of immunization against this viral disease cannot be exaggerated. Except for the natural resistance your animal carries against disease, it is the one means of protection you have against this killer. There have been various methods of immunization developed in the last several years, combining several vaccines in one. Injections can be given at any age, even as early as six or eight weeks, with a booster shot when recommended by your veterinarian. They do not affect the tissues, nor do they cause any ill effects to other dogs in a kennel who come in contact with the vaccinated animal.

Infectious Hepatitis

This disease attacks dogs of all ages, but is particularly deadly to puppies. We see young puppies in the nest, healthy, bright and sturdy; suddenly they begin to vomit, and the next day they are dead of infectious hepatitis; it strikes that quickly. The disease is difficult to diagnose correctly, and there is no specific treatment that will cure it. Astute authorities claim that if an afflicted dog survives three days after the onslaught of the disease he will, in all probability, completely recover. Treatment is symptomatic and directed at supporting the functions of the ailing liver. Prevention is through vaccination. Veterinarian vaccine programs usually combine distemper, hepatitis, and often leptospirosis vaccines.

Rabies

This is the most terrible of diseases, since it knows no bounds. It is transmissible to all kinds of animals and birds, including the superior animal, man. To contract this dread disease, the dog must be bitten by a rabid animal or the rabies virus must enter the body through a broken skin surface. The disease incubation period is governed by the distance of the virus' point of entry to the brain. The closer the point of entry is to the brain, the quicker the disease manifests itself. We can be thankful that rabies is not nearly as prevalent as is supposed by the uninformed. Restlessness, excitability, perverted appetite, character reversal, wildness, drowsiness, loss of acuteness of senses, and of feeling in some instances, foaming at the mouth, and many other lesser symptoms come with the onslaught of this disease. Diagnosis by trained persons of a portion of the brain is conceded to be the only way of determining whether an animal died of rabies or of one of the distemper complex diseases. Very little has been done in introducing drugs or specifics that can give satisfaction in combatting this disease, perhaps evaluation of the efficacy of such products is almost impossible with a disease so rare and difficult to diagnose.

Quarantine, such as that pursued in England, even of six-months' duration, is still not the answer to the rabies question, though it is undeniably effective. It is, however, not proof positive. Recently a dog on arriving in England was held in quarantine for the usual six months. The day before he was to be released to his owners, the attendant noticed that he was acting strangely He died the next day. Under examination his brain showed typical inclusion bodies, establishing the fact that he had died of rabies. This is a truly dangerous disease that can bring frightful death to animal or man. It should be the duty of every dog owner to protect his dog, himself, his family, and neighbors from even the slight risk that exists of contracting rabies by having his dog immunized. In many states immunization is compulsory.

FITS

Fits in dogs are symptoms of diseases rather than illness itself. They can be caused by the onslaught of any number of diseases, including worms, distemper, epilepsy, primary encephalitis, poisoning, etc. Running fits can also be traced to dietary deficiencies. The underlying reason for the fits, or convulsions, must be diagnosed by your veterinarian and the cause treated.

DIARRHEA

Diarrhea, a loose, watery movement, is often a symptom of one of many other diseases. But if, on taking your dog's temperature, you find there is no fever, it is quite possible the condition has been caused by either a change of diet, of climate or water, or even by a simple intestinal disturbance. A tightening agent such as Kaopectate should be given. Water should be withheld and corn syrup, dissolved in boiled milk, substituted to prevent dehydration in the patient. Feed hard-boiled eggs, boiled milk, beef, boiled white rice, cracker, kibbles, or dog biscuits. Add a tablespoonful of bone ash (not bone meal) to the diet. If the condition is not corrected within two or three days, if there is an excess of blood passed in the stool, or if signs of other illness become manifest, don't delay a trip to your veterinarian.

CONSTIPATION

If the dog's stool is so hard that it is difficult for him to pass it and he strains and grunts during the process, then he is obviously constipated. The cause of constipation is generally one of diet. Bones and dog biscuits, given abundantly, can cause this condition, as can any of the items of diet mentioned above as treatment for diarrhea. Chronic constipation can result in hemorrhoids which, if persistent, must be removed by surgery. The cure for constipation and its accompanying ills is the introduction of laxative food elements into the diet. Stewed tomatoes, buttermilk, skim milk, whey, bran, alfalfa meal, and various fruits can be fed and a bland physic given. Enemas can bring quick relief. Once the condition is alleviated, the dog should be given a good balanced diet, avoiding all types of foods that will produce constipation.

EYE AILMENTS

The eyes are not only the mirror of the soul, they are also the mirror of many kinds of disease. Discharge from the eyes is one of the many symptoms warning of most internal viral, helminthic, and bacterial diseases. Of the ailments affecting the eye itself, the most usual are: glaucoma, which seems to be a hereditary disease; pink eye, a strep infection; cataracts, opacity of the lens in older dogs; corneal opacity, such as follows some cases of infectious hepatitis; and teratoma or tumors. Mange, fungus, inturned lids, and growths on the lid are other eye ailments. The wise procedure is to consult your veterinarian for specific treatment.

When the eyes show a discharge from reasons other than those that can be labeled "ailment," such as irritation from dust, wind, or sand, they should be washed with warm water on cotton or a soft cloth. After gently washing the eyes, an ophthalmic ointment combining a mild anesthetic and antiseptic can be utilized. Butyn sulphate, one percent yellow oxide of mercury, and five percent sulphathiazole ointment are all good. Boric acid seems to be falling out of favor as an ophthalmic antiseptic. The liquid discharged by the dog's tear ducts is a better antiseptic, and much cheaper.

ANAL GLANDS

If your dog consistently drags his rear parts on the ground or bites this area, the cause is probably impacted anal glands. These glands, which are located on each side of the anus, should be periodically cleared by squeezing. The job is not a nice one, and can be much more effectively done by your veterinarian. Unless these glands are kept reasonably clean, infection can become housed in this site, resulting in the formation of an abscess which will need surgical care. Dogs that get an abundance of exercise seldom need the anal glands attended to.

The many other ailments which your dog is heir to, such as cancer, rupture, heart disease, fractures, and the results of accidents, etc., must all be diagnosed and tended to by your veterinarian. When you go to your veterinarian with a sick dog, always remember to bring along a sample of his stool for analysis. Many times samples of his urine are needed too. Your veterinarian is the only one qualified to treat your dog for disease, but protection against disease is, to a great extent, in the hands of the dog's owner. If those hands are capable, a great deal of pain and misery for both dog and owner can be eliminated. Death can be cheated, investment saved, and veterinary bills kept to a minimum. A periodic health check by your veterinarian is a wise investment.

We come now to a very controversial subject which is prominent in the minds of many dog fanciers at this time and so must be discussed here. The subject we mean is . . .

SUBLUXATION

First let us define the word. *Subluxation* means partial dislocation, or incomplete dislocation. As this partial dislocation refers to no specific section of the skeletal structure, subluxation means an incomplete dislocation of *any* joint. In common usage, however, this term has come to mean the partial dislocation of the femur and pelvis. It is in this more specific sense that it is used here. In this condition, the hip socket is shallow, allowing the femoral head, or ball part of the femur, to slip out of the socket partially or entirely. In the process of slipping, the femoral head becomes injured or flattened out, wearing to a flattened surface to compensate for the shallowness of the hip socket. The condition called coxa plana (coxa meaning hip joint and plana meaning flat) would seem to fit more closely the picture of what we call subluxation. Dorland's American Illustrated Dictionary defines coxa plana as "osteochondritis deformans juvenilis, a disease characterized by atrophy and rarefaction of the head of the femur during the age of growth, resulting in a shortened and thickened femoral neck and a broad, flat femoral head. Called also Perthes' disease, Calve-Perthes' disease, Legg's disease, pseudocoxalgia." Osteochondritis is an inflammation of both bone and cartilage. Coxa valga is defined as a deformity of the neck of the femur, producing in the limb marked external rotation, increased abduction, and decreased adduction.

To eliminate confusion, we will continue to call this condition subluxation, though as we progress it becomes clearer that it fits the definitions above more closely than it does the vague, all embracing definition of the word we use.

When the femoral head, flattened, begins to move from the shallow hip socket, the gristlelike capsule that surrounds this area thickens to hold the femur in place. The femoral head moves farther from the hip socket, becoming more deformed. Calcium deposits appear, filling in the gap. The area becomes inflamed, and an arthritic condition appears. Eventually the thickening of the capsule reaches a peak, as do the calcium deposits. When this occurs, the capsule breaks under stress, and the condition reaches a point

A dog's pulse can tell a veterinarian a great deal about his overall health. Every dog should have a regular annual veterinary checkup to be sure that he continues in good health. Photo by Louise Van der Meid.

where the afflicted animal must be destroyed.

The condition generally appears between the ages of three to twelve months and is thought to be congenital. There are a wide range of theories as to the basic cause of this ailment, ranging from individual intolerance of excess vitamin intake to undue stress upon the pelvic area due to excessive angulation. The latter theory can be almost ruled out entirely, since the incidence of subluxation is as prevalent in breeds not noted for acute angulation. In fact, Konde (1947) describes a subluxation of the coxo-femoral joint in German Shepherd dogs, which he reports is congenital and probably due to abnormal hip joints developed by breeding for long, low, extremely angulated rear quarters. Yet Moltzen-Nielson (1937) had formerly called what seems to be the same hip condition, in terriers, Calve-Perthes' disease, indicating that the condition is hereditary, but that the exact mode of inheritance is not known. Terriers, of course, are not noted for acute hindquarter angulation.

The theory most widely subscribed to at this time is that subluxation is both congenital and hereditary. In man the parallel ailment is considered to be the result of a recessive factor, and it is considered by many to be of the same origin in dogs. In litters which have come to our attention in which one or more puppies have shown the symptoms ascribed to the ailment, the ratios involved have not presented a clear genetic picture. This could be due to absorption of some of the fetuses before birth, early death of some of the young, or artificial culling of the litter. Whatever the cause, the percentage of affected individuals does not disclose the expected genetic ratio.

No real studies have been made of the mode of inheritance of the condition as it exists in dogs, assuming that it is an inheritable disease. If it is inheritable, it is still too early to come to any conclusion as to whether it is caused by recessive genes, masked dominants, or any other inheritable cause.

The condition can also be caused by an accident, a possibility which must not be overlooked. X-ray seems to be the only means of complete recognition of the condition. Yet the pliability of a puppy's bones and the position assumed by the puppy under X-ray can sometimes result in a picture that would seem to be the beginning of subluxation when it is not. A bitch brought to the Whitney Veterinary Clinic recently had a history of subluxation. She showed all the outward signs: the square hips, typical movement, and evidenced pain in the hind parts when she jumped or moved quickly. For reasons other than the manifestation of this ailment, she was subsequently destroyed. In the post mortem, the rear end of the animal was freed and the muscles cut away. But before muscles and ligaments were completely severed from the pelvic and upper femoral area, the movement of the femoral head in the hip socket was tested and seemed normal. When the femur and pelvis were bared, it was found that the hip socket was normally deep and the femoral head round, normal, and fitted snugly within the socket; there was no sign of subluxation. The bitch was then a year old. Undoubtedly there was something drastically wrong with this bitch which affected her hindquarters and her mode of locomotion, but it was not subluxation. Possibly the symptoms were due to a degeneration of certain nerves in the spinal column, and this could have been caused by injury or disease. The cause of her affliction could have been congenital or hereditary, or both. But we can only guess, with no real foundation of substantiating fact. Perhaps this was an isolated case, but if it wasn't, it gives us cause to wonder how many other dogs said to be subluxed, as was this bitch, fall into the same category as she does.

The picture of subluxation must take much more time and study before it comes into complete focus and absolute clarity is established. Until that time arrives, it would be best to keep our minds clear and receptive to new ideas and theories and not to condemn any particular animal or strain as carriers of the disease. If it is proven that subluxation is caused by a recessive gene or genes, as is now supposed, then remember that both parties to a breeding are equally to blame for the appearance of subluxed young in the nest box, because only individuals which carry a pair of determiners for a recessive trait will exhibit it, and the trait must come through both sire and dam for the puppies to inherit it.

ADMINISTERING MEDICATION

Some people seem to have ten thumbs on each hand when they attempt to give medicine to their dog. They become agitated and approach the task with so little sureness that their mood is communicated to the patient, increasing the difficulties presented. Invite calmness and quietness in the patient by emanating these qualities yourself. Speak to the animal in low, easy tones, petting him slowly, quieting him down in preparation. The administration of medicine should be made without fuss and as though it is some quiet and private new game between you and your dog.

At the corner of your dog's mouth there is a lip pocket perfect for the administering of liquid medicine if used correctly. Have the animal sit, then raise his muzzle so that his head is slanted upward looking toward the sky. Slide two fingers in the corner of his mouth where the upper and lower lip edges join, pull gently outward, and you have a pocket between the cheek flesh and the gums. Into this pocket pour the liquid medicine at the rate of approximately two tablespoonfuls at a time for a full-grown Weimaraner. Keep his head up, and the liquid will run from the pocket into his throat and he will swallow it. Continue this procedure until the complete dose has been given. This will be easier to accomplish if the medicine has been spooned into a small bottle. The bottle neck, inserted into the lip pocket, is tipped, and the contents drained at the ratio mentioned above.

To give pills or capsules, the head of the patient must again be raised with muzzle pointing upward. With one hand, grasp the cheeks of the dog just behind the lip edges where the teeth come together on the inside of the mouth. With the thumb on one side and the fingers on the other, press inward as though squeezing. The lips are pushed against the teeth, and the pressure of your fingers forces the mouth open. The dog will not completely close his mouth, since doing so would cause him to bite his lips. With your other hand, insert the pill in the patient's mouth as far back on the base of the tongue as you can, pushing it back with your second finger. Withdraw your hand quickly, allow the dog to close his mouth, and hold it closed with your hand, but not too tightly. Massage the dog's throat and watch for the tip of his tongue to show between his front teeth, signifying the fact that the capsule or pill has been swallowed.

In taking your dog's temperature, an ordinary rectal thermometer is adequate. It must be first shaken down, then dipped in vaseline, and inserted into the rectum for approximately three-quarters of its length. Allow it to remain there for no less than a full minute, restraining the dog from sitting completely during that time. When withdrawn, it should be wiped with a piece of cotton, read, then washed in alcohol—never hot water. The arrow on most thermometers at 98.6 degrees indicates normal human temperature and should be disregarded. Normal temperature for your grown dog is approximately 101 degrees; normal puppy temperature varies between $101\frac{1}{2}$ to 102 degrees. Excitement can raise the temperature, so it is best to take a reading only after the dog is calm.

In applying an ophthalmic ointment to the eye, simply pull the lower lid out, squeeze a small amount of ointment into the pocket thus produced, and release the lid. The dog will blink, and the ointment will spread over the eye.

Should you find it necessary to give your dog an enema, employ an ordinary human-size bag and rubber hose. For a Weimaraner a catheter is not necessary. Simply grease the rubber hose tip with vaseline and insert the hose well into the rectum. The bag should be held high for a constant flow of water. A quart of warm soapy water or plain water with a tablespoonful of salt makes an efficient enema.

FIRST AID

Emergencies quite frequently occur which make it necessary for you to care for the dog yourself until veterinary aid is available. Quite often emergency help by the owner can save the dog's life or lessen the chance of permanent injury. A badly injured animal, blinded to all else but abysmal pain, often reverts to the primitive wanting only to be left alone with his misery. Injured, panic-stricken, not recognizing you, he might attempt to bite when you wish to help him. Under the stress of fright and pain, this reaction is normal in animals. A muzzle can easily be slipped over his foreface, or a piece of bandage or strip of cloth can be fashioned into a muzzle by looping it around the dog's muzzle, crossing it under the jaws, and bringing the two ends around in back of the dog's head and tying them. Snap a leash onto his collar as quickly as possible to prevent him from running away and hiding. If it is necessary to lift him, grasp him by the neck, getting as large a handful of skin as you can, as high up on the neck as possible. Hold tight and he won't be able to turn his head far enough around to bite. Lift him by the hold you have on his neck until he is far enough off the ground to enable you to encircle his body with your other arm and support him or carry him.

Every dog owner should have handy a first-aid kit specifically for the use of his dog. It should contain a thermometer, surgical scissors, rolls of three-inch and six-inch bandage, a roll of one-inch adhesive tape, a package of surgical cotton, a jar of vaseline, enema equipment, bulb syringe, ten c.c. hypodermic syringe, flea powder, skin remedy, tweezers, ophthalmic ointment, paregoric, kaopectate, peroxide of hydrogen, merthiolate, a good antiseptic powder, alcohol, ear remedy, aspirin, milk of magnesia, castor oil, mineral oil, dressing salve.

We have prepared two charts for your reference, one covering general first-aid measures and the other a chart of poisons and antidotes. Remember that, in most instances, these are emergency measures, not specific treatments, and are designed to help you in aiding your dog until you can reach your veterinarian.

FIRST-AID CHART

Emergency	Treatment	Remarks
Accidents	Automobile, treat for shock. If gums are white, indicates probable internal injury. Wrap bandage tightly around body until it forms a sheath. Keep very quiet until veterinarian comes.	Call veterinarian immediately.
Bee stings	Give paregoric, 2 teaspoonfuls for grown Weimaraner, or aspirin to ease pain. If in state of shock, treat for same.	Call veterinarian for advice.
Bites (animal)	Tooth wounds: area should be shaved and antiseptic solution flowed into punctures with eye dropper. Iodine, merthiolate, etc., can be used. If badly bitten or ripped, take dog to your veterinarian for treatment.	If superficial wounds become infected after first aid, consult veterinarian.
Burns	Apply strong, strained tea to burned area, followed by covering of vaseline.	Unless burn is very minor, consult veterinarian immediately.
Broken bones	If break involves a limb, fashion splint to keep immobile. If ribs, pelvis, shoulder, or back involved, keep dog from moving until professional help comes.	Call veterinarian immediately.
Choking	If bone, wood, or any foreign object can be seen at back of mouth or throat, remove with fingers. If object can't be removed or is too deeply imbedded or too far back in throat, rush to veterinarian immediately.	

Cuts	Minor cuts: allow dog to lick and cleanse. If not within his reach, clean cut with peroxide, then apply merthiolate. Severe cuts: apply pressure bandage to stop bleeding—a wad of bandage over wound and bandage wrapped tightly over it. Take to veterinarian.	If cut becomes infected or needs suturing, consult veterinarian.
Dislocations	Keep dog quiet and take to veterinarian at once.	
Drowning	Artificial respiration. Lay dog on his side, push with hand on his ribs, release quickly. Repeat every 2 seconds. Treat for shock.	
Electric shock	Artificial respiration. Treat for shock.	Call veterinarian immediately.
Heat stroke	Quickly immerse the dog in cold water until relief is given. Give cold water enema. Or lay dog flat and pour cold water over him, turn electric fan on him, and continue pouring cold water as it evaporates.	Cold towels pressed against abdomen and back of head aid in reducing temp. quickly if quantity of water not available.
Porcupine quills	Tie dog up, hold him between knees, and pull all quills out with pliers. Don't forget tongue and inside of mouth.	See veterinarian to remove quills too deeply imbedded.
Shock	Cover dog with blanket. Allow him to rest and soothe with voice and hand.	Alcoholic beverages are NOT a stimulant. Bring to veterinarian.
Poisonous snake bite	Cut deep X over fang marks. Drop potassium permanganate into cut. Apply tourniquet above bite if on foot or leg.	Apply first aid only if a veterinarian or a doctor can't be reached.

TREATMENT FOR POISON

The important thing to remember when your dog is poisoned is that prompt action is imperative. Administer an emetic immediately. Mix hydrogen peroxide and water in equal parts. Force eight to ten tablespoonfuls of this mixture down your dog, or up to twelve tablespoonfuls (this dosage for a fully grown Weimaraner). In a few minutes he will regurgitate his stomach contents. Once this has been accomplished, call your veterinarian. If you know the source of the poison and the container which it came from is handy, you will find the antidote on the label. Your veterinarian will prescribe specific drugs and advise on their use.

The symptoms of poisoning include trembling, panting, intestinal pain, vomiting, slimy secretion from mouth, convulsions, coma. All these symptoms are also prevalent in other illnesses, but if they appear and investigation leads you to believe that they are the result of poisoning, act with dispatch as described above.

POISON	HOUSEHOLD ANTIDOTE
ACIDS	Bicarbonate of soda
ALKALIES	Vinegar or lemon juice
(cleansing agents)	
ARSENIC	Epsom salts
HYDROCYANIC ACID	Dextrose or corn syrup
(wild cherry; laurel leaves)	
LEAD	Epsom salts
(paint pigments)	
PHOSPHORUS	Peroxide of hydrogen
(rat poison)	
MERCURY	Eggs and milk
THEOBROMINE	Phenobarbital
(cooking chocolate)	
THALLIUM	Table salt in water
(bug poisons)	
FOOD POISONING	Peroxide of hydrogen, followed by enema
(garbage, etc.)	
STRYCHNINE	Sedatives. Phenobarbital, Nembutal.
DDT	Peroxide and enema

Chapter XV
The Weimaraner Standard

GENERAL APPEARANCE—A medium-sized, gray dog with light eyes, he should present a picture of great driving power, stamina, alertness and balance. Above all, the dog *should indicate ability to work hard in the field. Height*—Height at withers: dogs, 25 to 27 inches; bitches, 23 to 25 inches.

HEAD—Moderately long and aristocratic, with moderate stop and slight median line extending back over the forehead. Rather prominent occipital bone and trumpets set well back, beginning at the back of the eyesockets. Measurement from tip of nose to stop to equal that from stop to occipital bone. The flews should be moderately deep, enclosing a powerful jaw. Foreface perfectly straight, delicate at the nostrils. Skin tightly drawn. Neck cleancut and moderately long. Expression kind, keen, intelligent. *Ears*— Long and lobular, slightly folded and set high. The ear when drawn snugly alongside the jaw should end approximately two inches from the point of the nose. *Eyes*—In shades of light amber, gray or blue-gray, set well enough apart to indicate good disposition and intelligence. When dilated under excitement the eyes may appear almost black. *Teeth*—Well-set, strong and even; well-developed and proportionate to jaw with correct scissors bite, the upper teeth protruding slightly over the lower teeth but not more than $\frac{1}{16}$ of an inch. Complete dentition is greatly to be desired. *Nose*— Gray. *Lips and Gums*—Pinkish flesh shades.

BODY—The back should be moderate in length, set in straight line, strong, and should slope slightly from the withers. The chest should be well developed and deep, shoulder well laid on and snug. Ribs well sprung and long. Abdomen firmly held; moderately tucked-up flank. The brisket should drop to the elbow.

COAT—Short, smooth and sleek in shades of mouse-gray to silver-gray, usually blending to a lighter shade on the head and ears. Small white mark allowable on the chest, but not on any other part of the body. White spots that have resulted from injuries shall not be penalized.

LEGS—*Forelegs*—Straight and strong, with the measurement from the

George von Mit, U.D., N.R.D., owned by Helen and Jack Houle, and bred by George O'Mohundro. Sire: Dusty Hunter, II; dam: Anna Bea Hanna. Photo by Brown's.

elbow to the ground approximately equaling the distance from the elbow to the top of the withers. *Hindquarters*—Well-angulated stifles and straight hocks. Musculation well developed. *Feet*—Firm and compact, webbed, toes well arched, pads closed and thick, nails short and gray or amber in color. *Dewclaws*—Allowable only on forelegs, there optional.

TAIL—Docked. At maturity it should measure approximately six inches with a tendency to be light rather than heavy and should be carried in a manner expressing confidence and sound temperament.

GAIT—The walk is rather awkward. The trot should be effortless, ground covering and should indicate smooth co-ordination. When seen from the rear, the hind feet should parallel the front feet. When viewed from the side, the topline should remain strong and level.

TEMPERAMENT—The dog should display a temperament that is keen, fearless, friendly, protective and obedient.

VERY SERIOUS FAULTS

Any longhaired or coat darker than mouse-gray to silver-gray is considered a most undesirable recessive trait. White, other than a spot on chest. Eyes any other color than gray, blue-gray or light amber. Black, mottled mouth. Non-docked tail. Dogs exhibiting strong fear. Viciousness.

SERIOUS FAULTS

Poor gait. Very poor feet. Cowhocks. Faulty backs, either roached or sway. Badly overshot or undershot jaw. Snipy muzzle. Short ears. Yellow in white marking. Undersize.

FAULTS

Doggy bitches. Bitchy dogs. Improper muscular condition. Badly affected teeth. More than four missing teeth. Back too long or too short. Faulty coat. Neck too short, thick or throaty. Low tail set. Elbows in or out; feet east and west.

MINOR FAULTS

Tail too short or too long. Pink nose. Oversize should not be considered a serious fault, providing correct structure and working ability are in evidence.

Approved April 14, 1959

Chapter XVI
The Standard Discussed

A standard is a written analysis of a breed. The essence of its combined perfections present to the reader a word picture of a mythical superdog toward which the fancier must strive. In its entirety, the standard disciplines in selection and rejection toward an ethical center or objective, which is the betterment of the breed.

It was evidently the purpose of those who were instrumental in fashioning the standard to make it so clear and concise that the reader could, as closely as the written word permits, visualize the ideal. In this design they were eminently successful to the degree that such a document can be successful. Any failure of the reader to know our breed in all its detail does not reflect upon the standard. Rather, it can be blamed upon lack of visual imagination, or faulty interpretation of the written word by the reader. Standards can be too short or too vague, omitting succinct details that, in essence, differentiate the particular breed from all other breeds.

The standard, as it exists, is a worthwhile word picture of our breed. Interpretation of many of the passages is necessarily vague as to degree and can only be determined by comparison. In these instances, visual support is needed to fortify the script.

A standard should not be considered rigid and unchangeable. Time brings faults and virtues to a breed which must be recognized and the standard changed in certain particulars to accommodate new values. Since the standard is a yardstick for the show ring and the breeder, evaluation of new trends should be qualified not only by cosmetic application, but by genetic implication as well.

It is a pity that when a breed standard is devised, extensive scientific study is not readily available to determine the correlation of inherited characteristics to physical appearance. Relationship between genetic and physical manifestations have been found which should be studied before set standards are drawn up. It is difficult to eliminate one gene in a linked series without eliminating, or affecting, the other genes on the same chromosome.

Someday sufficient and conclusive enough proof will be established by exhaustive scientific research to enable us to chart correlations between linked

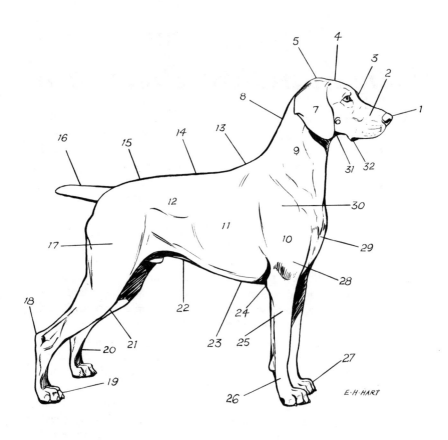

Parts of the Weimaraner

1. Nose 2. Muzzle 3. Stop 4. Skull 5. Occiput 6. Cheek 7. Ear 8. Crest of Neck 9. Neck 10. Shoulder 11. Ribs 12. Loin 13. Withers 14. Back 15. Croup 16. Tail or Stern 17. Thigh 18. Hock joint 19. Rear feet 20. Metatarsus 21. Stifle 22. Abdomen 23. Chest 24. Elbow 25. Foreleg 26. Pastern 27. Front feet 28. Upper arm 29. Forechest 30. Shoulder blade 31. Throat latch 32. Lip corner.

genetic and physical manifestations. We can then rewrite our standards to incorporate these associated characteristics and, by canny breeding, produce animals far superior to any known canine group of today.

The written standard of any breed can vary with individual interpretation. It is also quite possible for the novice to read the standard, compare it section by written section with his own animal, and come to the erroneous conclusion that their Weimaraner is perfect, conforming to the standard in every possible way.

 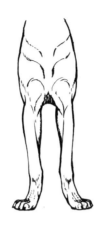 

1. Good front; 2. East and west, too narrow, pinched elbows; 3. Too heavy. Loaded shoulders. Out at elbows. Toes in. Too heavy in bone. Too broad in front.

Actually, when judging, one should balance virtues and not faults. But, when considering faults, those which are of genetic origin should be much more severely penalized than faults of a transitory nature such as lack of condition and poor coat, though these temporary faults may be more obvious to the gallery.

First, we must judge the dog as a complete entity, to assess the animal's overall balance and how his parts fit together. He must essentially have true breed type so that in no way could he be mistaken for any other breed of dog even were the basic and identifying breed color missing. An animal's parts, his head, neck, bone, front assembly, middle piece and rear quarter assembly may all, as individual sections, be superb. Yet it is quite possible that when assembled together in the same dog these near perfect sections may not fit properly and the dog will lack overall balance.

Faulty Specimen. Roman nose. Haw showing. Straight shoulders. Sway back. Too long in loin. Too high in tail-set. Sickle hocked. Coarse throughout.

The balance of weight to height, even though specified, can vary greatly in degree and so effect proportion. A heavy boned dog can be considered, by some judges, strongly boned and, by other judges, spongy, coarse or "wet." A lighter boned dog can be either "dry," of "dense" bone, or "too light" in bone, according to the judge who views the animal.

Even though we want a strong and powerful animal, a Weimaraner can be too muscular, cloddy, squat and heavy. Such animals are generally barrel chested, loaded in shoulders, short and thick in neck, toe in and are out at elbow when coming toward the judge, lack drive behind and overall floating ease in gait.

The antithesis of the above type is the tall, shallow, lightly boned animal that has neither substance or strength and is generally shallow chested, fiddle fronted, lacking in angulation both front and rear, and usually shows a tendency toward nervousness and flightiness.

Neither of these types is desirable but, of the two, the former is preferable. What we want in our "Gray Ghost" is elegance without weakness, and strength without coarseness. In movement, we want the ease that accompanies power and muscular tone and balance. Throughout, the dog should be clean-cut, noble and vigorous.

The Weimaraner's head is moderately long and lean, but not weak. The cheeks should be flat and the occiput clearly defined. The stop is neither as sharp or as deep as found in other pointing breeds. The muzzle is at least as long as the skull, flat on the sides, fairly deep and square. The appearance of squareness is aided by the cut of the flews, which should cover the lower jaw completely. The teeth should meet in the generally desirable "scissors" bite and should be complete in number, white and straight. The jaw should be deep and strong. Sometimes a puppy may be slightly overshot (upper set of teeth protruding too far beyond lower set), but this condition often rectifies itself upon maturity.

The light eyes are moderate in size and slightly almond in shape and are set in front of the brow and deeply enough to have a pleasing look. The rims of the eyes should fit tightly; the haw never be visually evident.

The ears of the Weimaraner are rather high set, hang flat against the cheek, are rather thin and pliable, and not too long or "houndy."

Faulty Specimen. Snipy muzzle. Dish faced. Loaded shoulders. Roach back. Down in pastern. Hare feet. Straight stifles. Too lightly built all over.

E. H. HART

The head should fit cleanly into the moderately long, slightly crested neck, showing no evidence of looseness ("wetness") or dewlap at the throat latch. The neck forms a graceful column into the front assembly, running smoothly into the high, dry wither.

The shoulder is set slightly back, not pushed too far forward as in most terriers and Great Danes. The flat shoulder blade (scapula), should form a ninety degree angle with the upper arm (humerus). Both bones should be as long as possible for the size of the dog, and both should be of approximately equal length. Outwardly the shoulders should be flat, not rounded with

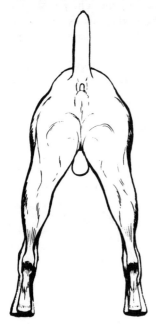 

E·H·H·

1. Good hindquarters.   2. Cow hocked; declaws on hind feet.

bulky muscle or fat. The front legs should be straight with a slight "give" in the pastern, not as exaggerated an angle as in the German Shepherd, nor as straight as in the Foxhound or most of the terriers. Feet, both front and rear, are well knuckled up and neat (front feet slightly larger than rear feet), with short, blunt claws and deep, thick pads.

The back, that section of the topline between the end of the high withers and the beginning of the croup, is short and strong. The "moderate" length of back mentioned in the Standard means that in overall length the Weimaraner must not be too cobby, too short or square. The croup should slope gently to the tail base. The long wither and rather long croup with the short

244

back between gives us a top-line that is moderate in length. If the back itself is too long it is usually weak, lacking firmness and often accompanied by a long, weak loin. A bitch can be slightly longer in back than a male, but if back and loin are too long, after a litter or two they weaken perceptively and the back will sag and bounce when the bitch is moving. The whole back assembly should form a very slight slope rearward to the tail set.

The ribs must be deep, carried well back and flattening slightly at the sides and toward the bottom as bone meets cartilage so that the animal will show a good spring of rib without the barrel formation that will interfere with the elbows when the dog moves. The prosternum (forechest bone) should be fairly obvious, jutting slightly beyond the shoulders when the dog is viewed in direct profile. The ribs should be deep enough so that the muscles sheathing them at the bottom should reach to the elbow or slightly deeper.

The loin, as mentioned earlier, should be short. It should also be fairly wide, deep, and powerful. The hindquarter assembly must exhibit power and muscularity, for this is the portion of the body which propels the dog forward during motion while the front assembly simply provides balance. Good angulation, a nice flair in stifle, and short strong hocks, which form a right angle to the floor when the dog is standing squarely on all fours, complement the heavy bands of muscle and strong tendons in the hindquarter assembly. Going away the hindquarters must move parallel without any indication of either cowhocks or bowed legs.

In movement your Weimaraner should exhibit both power and grace, smoothness and ease, with all parts complementing each other in effortless, balanced motion. The front legs must not lift high in the eye-catching hackney movement so often seen, and the hind legs must reach far under the dog and grip the ground firmly, then propel forward with power and vigor.

The "Gray Ghost," when off leash and working in the field, truly exhibits the floating, easy power of movement we want. Then, in his particular environment, he becomes a quicksilver flash of flowing movement: music, poetry in motion, the essense of canine beauty and strength molded to specific purpose.

Chapter XVII
The Future

What does the future hold for our breed? We are not seers, so we cannot predict the future. We can only review what has gone before and refrain from repeating the mistakes of the past or present and so find advancement in the time to come.

But, the author feels that the future of the Weimaraner is in the woods and water, in the fields with his master. There is his niche, there his usefulness to man, and toward this utilitarian purpose he must be bred.

Selection, rigid and devoid of sentimentality, must be made the tool to fashion the breed ever more purposely to this end. Competition in the field should become the measurement of ability in the individual, and his worth in future breeding plans assessed by this yardstick of performance. We must press always toward perfection in this area of endeavor. The popularity, the future, of the Weimaraner rests on his ability as a gun dog.

Do we want to fashion him to compete against other gun dogs in field trials, seeking the glory of winning in competition against other fine sporting breeds? Or do we want to keep him confined to the acre in which he was originally conceived: as a gentleman's gun dog and companion in the hunt?

In the final analysis the future of the Weimaraner is up to you, the owners and breeders. You must carry the responsibility for molding the future of the breed. New theories, new techniques, new discoveries are constantly being made in the many fields of scientific endeavor. Never-ending research uncovers new concepts in canine medicine, nutrition, physiology, psychology, and genetics. Immunities and cures are in the process of development which will destroy diseases that today take a terrible toll. Under the microscope and in the testing kennel old problems are being met and defeated. Geneticists probe ever deeper into the why of being, giving us, if we will but look for them, new answers to our breeding problems. We must face this future with open minds and with tolerance. We must learn to understand new concepts and avoid harking back blindly to the incomplete knowledge and patterns of the past.

Yesterday's miracles are the mundane, accepted facts of tomorrow, and the wonders of today are but the stepping stones to far greater wonders to come.

Ch. Miss Deborah of Wetobe, owned and handled by Mrs. H. B. Barnett, after scoring an important win. She is typical of the fine Weimaraners bred in the United States at the present day. Photo by Alexander.

This then is the future; a time when fresh, new tools will be made available for our use with which we can better shape the destiny of our breed, if we will but use them, and use them well.

The past has brought, in many instances, doubts that our "Gray Ghosts" could live up to the publicity that preceded them. Let the future erase those doubts and bring even more concrete evidence of the Weimaraner's worth.

Yes, the future is in your hands. If they are knowing and sure and capable they will shape the destiny of the breed to the ever greater glory it deserves.

THE END

GLOSSARY

of Pertinent German Words, Terms, and Abbreviations

Translations from German Pedigrees

Rude	male	*W.T.-Wurf Tag*	date whelped
Hundin	female	*Z.-Zuchter*	breeder
Wurf	litter	*B.-Besitzer*	owner
Welpe	young puppy	*A.-Amme*	foster mother
Eltern	parents	*V.-Vater*	sire (father)
Gross Eltern	grandparents	*M.-Mutter*	dam (mother)
Ur-Gross Eltern	great-grandparents	*S.Z.*	stud book
Gedeckt	date of mating	*Angekoert*	recommended for breeding

German Show Ratings

V.A.	Select Class	*A.-Ausreishend*	Sufficient
V.-Vorzuglich	Excellent	*M.-Mangelhaft*	Faulty
S.G.-Sehr Gut	Very Good	*O.-Zero*	Failed, N.G.
G.Gut	Good	*Auslese Klass*	Selection Class (See *V.A.*)

Sr.-Sieger	German Grand Champion
Sgrn.-Siegerin	German Grand Champion

German Working Dog Ratings

P.H.-Polizei Hund	police dog
H.G.H.-Herden Gebrauchshund	herding dog
Bl.H.-Blinden Hund	blind guide dog
S.H.-Such Hund	tracking dog
F.H.-Fahrten Hund	trailing dog
D.H.-Dienst Hund	service dog
S.H.-Sanitats Hund	Red Cross dog
Gr.H.-Grenzen Hund	border patrol dog
M.H.-Militar Hund	army dog
Law.H.-Lawinen Hund	avalanche dog
Sch.H.-Schutz Hund	protection dog
Kr.H.-Kriegshund	war dog
Z.Pr.-Zucht prufung	has passed Breed Survey and is recommended for breeding
Leistung	field training
Leistungssieger and *Leistungssiegerin*	all around working dog (field trial) champions of the year in their sex.

German Show Classes

J.Kl.-Jugend Klasse	youth class, 12 to 18 months.
J.H.Kl.-Junghund Klasse	young dog class, 18 to 24 months.
G.H.Kl.-Gebrauchshund Klasse	dogs with Sch. 1, 2, or 3 training degrees over 2 years of age.
A.Kl.-Alters Klasse	dogs of over 2 years of age with no training degrees.

Bei Fuss	Heel!	*Bleib*	Stay!
Setz	Sit!	*Gib laut*	Speak!
Platz	Down!	*Pass auf*	On the alert!
Komm	Come!	*Fass*	Attack!
Such	Go find! (Search!	*Pfui*	Shame! No!
	Seek!)	*Hoch* ⎫	Up! Over! (command for
Vorwarts	Go Ahead!	*Hopp* ⎰	jumping)
Apport	Fetch!	*Hier*	Here! Come here!
Bringen	To fetch	*Gradaus*	Forward!
Auf	Up!	*Lass*	Let Go!
Aus	Out! Let go!	*Legen*	Lie down!
Daun	Down! Drop!	*Bleibsitzen*	Stay! Remain sitting!

Wasserhundprufung	Water dog trial
Deutsche Pointer u. Setter Verein	German Pointer and Setter Club
Zur Spur	Trail
Leistungbuch	Trial register book
Leistungprufung	Field trial
Paar	Brace, pair.

Glossary of genetic terms and symbols

1. ALLELE (*noun*). Either of a pair of genes, factors, traits. See Allelomorphs.
2. ALLELOMORPHS (*noun; adj.* allelomorphic). Unlike genes, factors, traits, or types of a given pair. Contrasting gene pattern.
3. AUTOSOMES (*noun; adj.* autosomal). Paired, ordinary chromosomes, similar in both sexes, as differentiated from the sex chromosomes.
4. CHROMOSOMES (*noun*). Small microscopic bodies within the cells of all living things. When division of cells begins the chromosomes appear as rods or short strings of beads.
5. CROSSING-OVER (*noun*). An exchange of inheritance factors or genes between related chromosomes.
6. DOMINANT (*noun* or *adj.*). A trait or character that appears. Indicates that a trait contributed by one parent conceals a somewhat different trait from the other parent.
7. EPISTASIS (*noun; adj.* epistatic). Like dominance, but epistasis occurs between factors not alternative or allelomorphic. An epistatic gene masks the effect of genes that are not its allele or partner.
8. F_1. Represents the first filial generation. The progeny, or "get," produced from any specific mating.
9. F_2. Is the symbol used to denote the second filial generation, that is, the progeny, or young, produced from a mating of a male and female from the F_1 breeding above.
10. FACTOR (*noun*). A simple Mendelian trait: may be considered synonymous with gene.
11. GENE (*noun*). A single unit of inheritance (Mendel's "Determiners"); a microscopic part of a chromosome.
12. GENOTYPE (*noun; adj.* genotypic). The hereditary composition of an individual. The sum total of every dog's dominant and recessive traits.

13. GET. Puppies or offspring.

14. HETEROZYGOUS (*adj.*). Possessing contrasting genes (or allelomorphs). Where dominant and recessive genes are both present for any trait or traits.

15. HOMOZYGOUS (*adj.*). Pure for a given trait, or possessing matched genes for that trait. The opposite of heterozygous. (Thus inbred strains are said to be homozygous, and outcrossed strains to be heterozygous. Degree must be substantiated.)

16. HYPOSTASIS (*noun; adj.* hypostatic). The masking of the effect of a gene by another gene not its allele. The hypostatic gene is the one masked. See epistasis. Not an allelomorph.

17. PHENOTYPE (*noun; adj.* phenotypic). The external appearance of an individual. The outward manifestation of all dominant genetic material (or double recessives). See Recessive.

18. RECESSIVE (*noun* or *adj.*). A trait or character that is concealed by an equivalent dominant character. Exception: when no dominant is present and two recessive genes pair to produce a certain trait.

19. ♂. Indicates a male. The symbol represents the shield and spear of Mars, the god of war.

20. ♀. Indicates a female. This symbol represents the mirror of the goddess of love, Venus.

21. X . Means "with," "between," etc. A mating between any male and female.

BIBLIOGRAPHY

Arenas, N., and Sammartino, R., Le Cycle Sexuel de la Chienne. *Etude Histol. Bull. Histol. Appl. Physiol. et Path.*, 16:299, 1939.

Ash, E. C., *Dogs: Their History and Development*, 2 vols., London, 1927.

Anrep, G. V., "Pitch Discrimination in the Dog." *J. Physiol.*, 53:376-85, 1920.

Barrows, W. M., *Science of Animal Life*. New York, World Book Co., 1927.

Burns, Marca, 1952. The Genetics of the Dog, Comm. Agri. Bur., Eng. 122 pp.

Castle, W. E., *Genetics and Eugenics*, 4th ed. Cambridge, Mass., Harvard University Press, 1930.

Darwin, C., *The Variation of Animals and Plants Under Domestication*, New York, D. Appleton Co., 1890.

Davenport, C. B., *Heredity in Relation to Eugenics*. New York, Henry Holt & Co., Inc., 1911.

Dorland, W. A. N., A.M., M.D., F.A.C.S., *The American Illustrated Medical Dictionary*. Philadelphia, W. B. Saunders Co., 1938.

Duncan, W. C., *Dog Training Made Easy*. Boston, Little, Brown & Co., 1940.

Dunn, L. C., and Dobzhansky, T., *Heredity, Race and Society*. New York, New American Library of World Litrature, 1946.

Elliot, David D., *Training Gun Dogs to Retrieve*. New York, Henry Holt & Co., 1952.

Evans, H. M., and Cole, H. H., "An Introduction to the Study of the Oestrus Cycle of the Dog." *Mem. Univ. Cal.*, Vol. 9, No. 2.

Fehringer (Prof.), St. Hubertus Brachen, *Unser Hund*, 1940.

Hart, E. H., "Artificial Insemination." *Your Dog*, March, 1948.

———— "The Judging Situation," *Your Dog*, March, 1948.

———— Doggy Hints. *Men Mg.* Zenith Pub. Co., 1950.

———— "Judgment Day." *Shep. Dog Rev.*, Jan., 1953.

———— *This is the Puppy*, T.F.H. Publications, Inc., 1962.

———— *Budgerigar Handbook*, T.F.H. Pub. Inc., 1960.

———— and Goldbecker, *This is the German Shepherd*, T.F.H. Pub., Inc., 1955.

Herber, Robert a.d. (Major), *The Weimaraner* (Germany). *The Weimaraner*, Deutsche Waidwerk, No. 22, Sept. 1, 1939.

Hermansson, K. A., "Artificial Impregnation of the Dog." *Svensk. Vet. Tidshr.*, 39:382, 1934.

Humphrey, E. S. "Mental Tests for Shepherd Dogs." *J. of Hered.*, 25:129, 1934.

————, and Warner, Lucien, *Working Dogs*. Baltimore, Johns Hopkins Press, 1934.

Ilger, Emil, Weimaraner Pointer, *Gebrauchs und Luxushunde*, 1922.

Keeler, C. E., and Trimble, H. C., "Inheritance of Dewclaws." *J. of Hered.*, 29:145, 1938.

Kelly, G. L., and Whitney, L. F., Prevention of Conception in Bitches by Injections of Estrone, *J. Ga. Med. Assoc.*, 29:7, 1940.

Kraus, C., Beitrag zum Prostatakrebs und Kryptorchismus des Hundes. *Frankfurter Zeitsch. Path.*, 41:405, 1931.

Krushinsky, L. A., "A Study of the Phenogenetics of Behaviour Characters in Dogs." *Biol. Journ. T.*, VII, No. 4, Inst. Zool., Moscow State Univ., 1938.

Laughlin, H. H., "Racing Capacity of Horses." Dept. of Genetics 37-73. Yearbook, Carn. Inst. No. 30, *The Blood Horse*, 1931.

Linke, J. Carl, *Unser Jagdhund*, Vol. 4, No. 26.

MacDowell, E. C., "Heredity of Behaviour in Dogs," Dept. of Genetics, *Yearbook*, Carn. Inst., No. 20, 101-56, 1921.

Muller, Friedrich, *Geschichte des Verein fur Deutsche Schaferhunde*. 1899-1949. S.V., Augsburg, 1949.

Nagel, W. A., Der Farbensinn des Hundes. *Zbl. Physiol.*, 21, 1907.

Otto, E. von, Grey Pointers of Weimar, *Huntsport und Jagd*. 1930.

Pearson, K., and Usher, C. H., "Albinism in Dogs." *Biometrica*, 21:144-163, 1929.

Razran, H. S., and Warden, C. J., "The Sensory Capacities of the Dog (Russian Schools)." *Psychol. Bulletin* 26, 1929.

"R.F.", Origin of the Weimaraner, *Deutsche Waidwerk*, No. 19, 1939.

Roesbeck, Dr., 40 *Jahre Arbeit fur den Deutschen Schaferhunde*, S.V., Augsburg, 1939.

Stetson, J., "Heartworm Can Be Controlled." *Field and Stream*, June 1954.

Stroese, Dr. A., Weimaraners, *Unser Hund*, 1902.

Whitney, L. F., *The Basis of Breeding*. N. H. Fowler, 1928.

——— *How To Breed Dogs*. New York, Orange Judd Pub. Co., 1947.

——— *Feeding Our Dogs*. New York, D. van Nostrand Co. Inc., 1949.

——— *Complete Book of Dog Care*, Garden City, L.I., Doubleday & Co. Inc., 1953.

——— and Whitney, G. D., *The Distemper Complex*. Orange, Conn., Practical Science Pub. Co., 1953.

INDEX